ational Waterways Conference Map

THE ORIGIN AND DEVELOPMENT OF THE WATERWAYS POLICY OF THE UNITED STATES

The Origin and Development of the Waterways Policy of the United States

BY
WILLIAM J. HULL
AND ROBERT W. HULL

NATIONAL WATERWAYS CONFERENCE, INC.
Washington
1967

Dedication

TO THE MEMORY of Paul G. Blazer (1890-1966), of Ashland, Kentucky, the first President and one of the founders of the National Waterways Conference, Inc., this essay is respectfully dedicated. Thus, we would accord a measure of recognition, however inadequate, to Mr. Blazer's unique contribution to public understanding of the relevance of American waterways policy to the economic development of the Nation.

It is with profound gratitude for his helpful guidance and the highest esteem for his wisdom and insight, so generously shared, that we offer this tribute to his memory.

Acknowledgements

TO James E. Moss of Washington, D. C., for his brilliant original work on *Internal Improvements* which brought together from Presidential messages and other original documents the main themes of American waterways policy; to Professor Marvin J. Barloon of the Department of Economics, Case-Western Reserve University, Cleveland, Ohio, for invaluable assistance on the analyses of economic issues; and to Harry N. Cook, Managing Director of the National Waterways Conference, Inc., and his staff for diligent editorial assistance.

Preface

THE RIVERS and streams of America have had a profound influence on the course of our history. Where once their rampaging waters menaced every valley, the waterways are today one of our greatest national assets. This dramatic transformation has resulted from the vision of early statesmen, the dreams of a struggling people, and a sound, far-sighted policy conceived and developed by the Congress over a period of many decades.

This volume records the men and events, down through the years, which came together to shape American waterways policy into a potent force serving the public good. This well-researched and documented study fills a need long recognized among students of history, government and economics. It should be of great benefit to all those engaged in formulating policy for future generations.

In these pages will be found a listing of the sources and authorities relevant to the origin and development of the waterways policy which guides us today. This compilation, in itself, should be helpful to students and policy-makers alike in conveying a better understanding of the public values of water resource development and low-cost water transportation.

This book also puts our waterways policy into an historical setting indicating the central role it has played to this day in the development of the Nation and its conscious use by the Congress as an instrument in achieving national goals in the fields of commerce, industry and economics. An established waterways policy is firmly embedded in our national life as a means of promoting important public objectives – such as dispersal of industry to interior sections and regional economic development. It offers even greater promise of usefulness in meeting the challenges of tomorrow.

As an artery of transportation, waterways are modern and progressive. Barges plying the 25,000-mile inland waterways system transport nearly 10 percent of all the freight moving between U. S. cities. In recent years, we have seen tremendous technological advances in the barge and towing industry, giving water transportation an even greater potential for the future than ever before.

Moreover, navigation plays a vital role in comprehensive water resource development for flood control, water quality control, water supply, recreation and many other essential purposes. Impairment of the navigation element of multiple-purpose projects or programs would hamper attainment of these water resource objectives.

It would be folly to impair the usefulness of the waterways system—in any of its many worthwhile public aspects—by repudiating established national policy. If there is a lesson from history, it is that the toll-free waterways policy has helped to build America. In the years ahead, adherence to the tested precepts of established waterways policy can exercise a powerful and beneficent influence on our future.

William Hull has performed an outstanding public service in bringing to the attention of the public the history and potential of our national waterways system.

> SENATOR STEPHEN M. YOUNG
> Chairman, Flood Control-Rivers
>   and Harbors Subcommittee of
>   the Senate Public Works Committee.

Washington, D. C.
May, 1967

CONTENTS

THE ORIGIN AND DEVELOPMENT OF THE WATERWAYS POLICY OF THE UNITED STATES

Taxation is old as time and takes its earliest form in the action of the petty chief who builds himself a stockade at the estuary, the river junction or mountain pass and levies a toll on the passing traveler or merchant.

C. NORTHCOTE PARKINSON
The Law and the Profits, p. 22

AMERICAN NATIONAL POLICY calling for free use of the Nation's rivers, harbors, lakes and other watercourses and their improvement by the National Government for the general welfare had its origin in the crucial struggle to block and reverse the divisive forces tending toward destruction of the Union in the aftermath of the Revolution and to save the Trans-Appalachian West for the United States.[1]

I. Freedom of the Waterways — Origins

No sooner had the United States won independence than commercial rivalries and sectionalism threatened to disintegrate the new Nation whose independence had been so dearly won by the sacrifice and devotion of a united people.[2]

The lack of central authority to regulate commerce was one of the major defects of the Articles of Confederation under which the National Government operated until 1789. Retaliatory trade wars among the States grew in intensity. "New York, for example, profiting by her port of entry, laid duties upon incoming commerce destined for New Jersey and Connecticut, while these States in turn taxed interstate commerce with New York."[3]

1

The problem of trade rivalry and discrimination was therefore of central concern to delegates to the Constitutional Convention assembled in Philadelphia in 1787. They were mindful not only of the destructive commercial rivalries besetting the Confederation but of imposts on water commerce of the type which had hampered the trade of Europe and denied to the nations of the Old World the benefits of the great waterways with which they had been richly endowed.

Thus, Alexander Hamilton noted in *The Federalist:*

> The commerce of the German Empire is in continual trammels from the multiplicity of the duties which the several princes and states exact upon the merchandise passing through their territories, by means of which the fine streams and navigable rivers with which Germany is so happily watered are rendered useless. Though the genius of the people of this country might never permit this description to be strictly applicable to us, yet one may reasonably expect, from the gradual conflicts of State regulations, that the citizens of each would at length come to be considered and treated by the others in no better light than that of foreigners and aliens.[4]

Hamilton's fear of sectional discrimination and duties on navigation was shared by other early American leaders. Several delegates to the Constitutional Convention expressed their anxieties regarding State imposts on commerce and obstructions to navigation on the Mississippi River.[5]

The lessons learned from the commercial chaos and sectional antagonism of the Confederation were translated into the great constitutional guaranties designed to protect commerce from discriminatory burdens and to preserve sectional balance: the Commerce Clause itself granting to Congress the exclusive power to regulate interstate commerce,[6] the accompanying prohibitions against discriminatory taxation[7] and port preferences,[8] State tonnage duties[9] and taxes on imports,[10] and the ban upon Federal and State duties on exports.[11]

Specifically with regard to the Trans-Appalachian West, regional rivalries were endangering the hold of the original States upon this vast region. Both England and Spain and later France, occupying the flanks of the Old West and supporting Indian depredations on the frontiers, early sought to encourage the forces of disunion and to lop off the disaffected settlements from the original States.[12] Indifference or positive opposition to western interest on the part of the northeastern States, particularly New England, came close to casting the West adrift in the mid-1780's. A commercial treaty with Spain was urgently desired by northern merchants who were willing that the United States should, in return, agree not to use the Mississippi River for 25 years. Settlers of the South and West were violently opposed. The issue threatened the Union.

Fortunately for the future, George Washington, preeminent among American leaders, fully recognized the gravity of this threat. Thus, in 1784, he travelled to the Ohio country seeking a trade route which could tie the West to the Eastern Seaboard and thus halt the accelerating drift toward disunion.[14] Commercially effective transportation under the conditions of the time and with the vast distances involved, required a route over the greater portion of which carriage by water was possible.[15] Freedom of navigation from obstructive tolls or taxes became, therefore, an integral element in any effective plan for improving commercial ties between East and West in the interest of national unity.

As noted above, Hamilton had commented in *The Federalist* with regard to the hampering effect upon commerce of waterway tolls or duties. The vast distances to be traversed by goods moving from interior points to salt water in North America had led to early introduction of freedom of navigation into the public law of the Continent. Thus, the Treaty of Paris of 1763 among France, Great Britain and Spain which ceded to Great Britain the territory of Louisiana lying east of the Mid-Channel of the Mississippi River (except "the Isle of Orleans") provided for mutual liberty of navigation from the source to the sea and stipulated that there be freedom from payment of tolls.[16] The Treaty of Paris of 1783 between the United States and Great Britain reaffirmed this principle, as it guaranteed that fluvial navigation from source to sea was to remain forever free and open to the subjects of Great Britain and the citizens of the United States.[17]

But the famous Ordinance of 1787 for the government of the Northwest Territory (the region north of the Ohio River and east of the Mississippi River and including present-day Ohio, Indiana, Illinois, Michigan, Wisconsin and part of Minnesota) is justifiably regarded as the cornerstone of the free waterway policy of the United States.

During the same summer when the delegates to the Constitutional Convention were drafting the Constitution of the United States, the last Congress of the old Confederation, meeting in New York, "was by one final and spasmodic burst of energy erecting one of the major pillars of constitutional doctrine upon which the future of the United States was most to depend."[18]

A group of New England veterans of the Revolutionary War, seeking to purchase western land for the depreciated certificates which they had earned in lieu of payment for their services, under the leadership of three Revolutionary War generals — Rufus Putnam and Benjamin Tupper of Massachusetts, and Samuel Parsons of Connecticut, with the Reverend Manasseh Cutler as their chief negotiator, were successful in persuading Congress to adopt a plan for government of the national territory northwest of the Ohio into which the new Ohio Company proposed to introduce settlers.[19]

New England members . . . who had tolerated their southern colleagues' western interests only in return for an equivalent toleration of their own fishing and commercial interests, were now taking the lead in advocating this new expansion project. . . . Most effective of all in capturing Congressional attention was the prospect after so many profitless years of making so considerable a land sale. . . .

For all its haste Congress had composed a remarkably comprehensive document establishing precedents as fundamental as those in the Constitution then under construction. It had established a government for a wilderness where government had never before existed. For the first time authority to govern a portion of the people of the United States had been vested not in the government of a state but in the government of the union of the states. Also for the first time the great doctrine of the admission of new states had been firmly implanted as a permanent and principal covenant in that union. Most significant of all, the people of the several states had been given that common and mutual interest which Washington in 1784 had considered a necessity were the union to endure. It had at last been made apparent that the people of Massachusetts or Connecticut could have the same interest in the projection of the United States westward into the Mississippi Valley as had the people of Virginia or the Carolinas. . . .

. . . In those four crowded July days Congress had been inspired as though by a vision of the future growth of the United States to open and guard the way to that stupendous achievement.

But the drafters of the great Ordinance did not limit their efforts to a mere general outline of the American West that was to be. They attended also to every detail. *Provision was made for* the conveyance of property, the *freedom of navigation,* the qualification of voters, and the organization of counties. A complete and specific bill of rights was included. Freedom of religion was guaranteed. Land was set aside to support public education. On the initiative of Virginia, future limitations were placed on slavery. In sum, the Ordinance made it possible for any American who henceforth sought a new home in the wilderness northwest of the Ohio to feel confident that he might remain an American whose every American right and privilege was surely protected under a local government as responsible to him as had been the one he had left.[20] (Emphasis supplied)

The Navigation Clause itself deserves special comment. The background of this clause embodied in Article IV of the Ordinance affords clear evidence that its framers gave close attention to every principle of public policy that could affect the future welfare of that region. It was extremely important to Manasseh Cutler and his associates of the Ohio Company to secure absolute freedom of "waters and carrying places," as that was the only means of effective transportation for commerce between the interior and the Eastern Seaboard. [21]

By a letter of March 8, 1785, from Colonel Timothy Pickering to Rufus King, one of the authors of the Ordinance of 1787, Colonel Pickering had noted that a proposed ordinance then under consideration for the government of the Northwest Territory contained no provision concerning navigation and, with regard to this omission, he said:

Water communications in that country will always be in the highest degree interesting to its inhabitants. It seems very necessary to secure the freedom of navigating the rivers to all the inhabitants of all the States. [22]

George Washington himself made it clear that he recognized the value of unhindered water transportation between the Atlantic seaboard and the western country. In a letter to Colonel Humphries on July 25, 1785, Washington wrote:

My attention is more immediately engaged in a project which, I think big with great political as well as commercial consequences to the States, especially the middle ones; it is by removing obstructions and extending the inland navigation of our rivers, to bring the States on the Atlantic in close connection with those forming to the westward by a short and easy transportation. [23]

As a result of the impetus provided by these men and other framers of the Ordinance, such as Richard Henry Lee of Virginia, Nathan Dane of Massachusetts and Edward Harrington of Virginia, it established freedom of the waterways in these words:

> The navigable waters leading into the Mississippi and St. Lawrence, and the carrying places between the same, shall be common highways and forever free, as well to the inhabitants of said territory as to citizens of the United States, and those of other States that may be admitted into the confederacy, without any tax, impost, or duty therefor. (Article IV) [24]

Articles I through VI of the Ordinance of 1787 are, by virtue of the preamble thereto, established as a solemn compact in these terms:

> It is hereby ordained and declared by the authority aforesaid, that the following articles shall be considered as articles of compact between the original States and the people and States in the said territory, and forever remain unalterable except by common consent.

By an Act of Congress on August 7, 1789, one of the first under the new Constitution of the United States, the Ordinance of 1787 was adopted without change. [25] This act provided the legal foundation for the free waterways policy of the United States during the nineteenth and twentieth centuries. As pointed out in a note in the *Wisconsin Law Review*:

> The general rule that the Ordinance of 1787 is inoperative except as an aid in construction deserves qualification in regard to Article IV dealing with navigable waters and carrying places which enjoys peculiar force because later decisions hold it still in force as a regulation of commerce. [26]

After Congress had adopted the Ordinance of 1787 as a statute of the United States, it then extended to the inhabitants of the Southwest Territory by the Ordinance of May 26, 1790, the "privileges, benefits and advantages" of the Northwest Ordinance. As a result of this extension, Article IV of the Compact of the Ordinance of 1787 pertained directly to the rights of Kentucky, Tennessee and Alabama as well as to the rights of Ohio, Michigan, Indiana, Illinois, Wisconsin, Minnesota (east of the Mississippi River) and Pennsylvania (that part included in the Erie Purchase).

To underscore the free waterways policy of the Ordinance, the language of Article IV was incorporated in the constitutions of many States admitted to the Union after 1790 [27] and the same or similar provisions were included by Congress in many of the enabling acts admitting new States to the Union. [28]

In conjunction with these acts of admission which stipulated that the navigable waters of particular States were to remain free from tolls, imposts or duties, Congress enacted, on March 3, 1803, that all navigable rivers within the United States territory to be disposed of south of the State of Tennessee should be deemed to be and remain public highways. [29]

This interest of the Congress in assuring the free navigation of the rivers of the Nation received great impetus from the inhabitants of the western regions. During the 1790's these western settlers were gravely concerned by the Spanish and French threats to American navigation of the Mississippi River. It was apparent during this crucial, formative phase of the Union that the western settlers might have been willing to accept the allegiance of another country rather than lose their right to free navigation of the Mississippi. [30] The necessity of guaranteeing the continued free navigation of the Mississippi in order to reassure the restive inhabitants of the South and West that their rights would be protected, played a major role in Thomas Jefferson's decision to purchase the Louisiana Territory from France in 1803. [31] President Jefferson was well aware of the threat which French possession of New Orleans posed to the stability of the United States, and he determined to establish the cohesion of the Union by bringing unity to the Mississippi Valley. [32]

After the Louisiana Purchase, America's right to the free use of the Mississippi River was never again seriously questioned. [33] President Tyler expressed the accepted view concerning its free status in public law and the importance of freedom of navigation in motivating the Louisiana Purchase in his veto message of June 11, 1844, as follows:

> The Mississippi River belongs to no particular State or States, but of common right, by express reservation, to all the States. It is reserved as a great common highway for the commerce of the whole Country. To have conceded to Louisiana or to any other State admitted as a new State into the Union, the exclusive jurisdiction, and consequently the right to make improvements and

levy tolls on the segments of the river embraced within its terri-
torial limits, would have been to have disappointed the chief object in the purchase of Louisiana, which was to secure the free
use of the Mississippi River to all the people of the United States.

Whether levies on commerce were made by a foreign or domestic government would have been equally burdensome and
objectionable.

Thus, the guiding principle of freedom of navigation
emerged from the geographical, economic and political neces-
sities of the new Nation. A Nation of continental expanse required cheap transportation; preservation of the Union and
the economic welfare and growth of the Nation demanded an
end to sectional rivalries with their attendant burdens on commerce and trade; facility of communication and ease and economy of transport were prerequisites for holding and defending
the Trans-Appalachian West against the depredations of foreign
powers and the splintering tendencies of the remote frontier.
Much the same combination of influences operated to forge the
principle of Federal responsibility for waterway improvements.

II. Federal Improvement Policy — Origins

There was abroad in the Nation well before the adoption of the Constitution a spirit of public improvement which carried with it, in the eyes of Washington and many others, a duty incumbent both upon governments and individual citizens to develop the Country's natural advantages by improvements in transportation.[34]

Writing in *The Federalist,* James Madison, John Jay and Alexander Hamilton emphasized the importance and necessity of Federal improvement of transportation facilities. Madison was of the opinion that:

> Nothing which tends to facilitate the intercourse between the States can be deemed unworthy of the public care.[35]

And further Madison said:

> . . . Intercourse throughout the Union will be facilitated. . . . The communications between the western and the Atlantic districts and between various parts of each will be rendered more and more easy by those numerous canals with which the beneficence of nature has intersected our Country and which art finds it so little difficult to connect and complete.[36]

As mentioned above, Jay and Hamilton expressed their views in a similar vein in *The Federalist* [37] and Hamilton enunciated his views further in his 1791 *Report on Manufactures.*[38] Hamilton believed that the economic development and prosperity of the Country were dependent upon the improvement of inland navigation. Although Hamilton viewed the improvement of the Nation's navigation facilities as most worthy of the cares of local governments, he considered this to be one of

9

those improvements which could be prosecuted with more efficacy by the whole than by any part or parts of the Union. The policy of internal improvements also found support in action taken by the First Congress in 1789 authorizing the Federal Treasury to assume the costs of lighthouses, beacons, buoys and public piers which had been erected by the Colonial governments.[39]

While the Ordinance of 1787, the adoption of the Constitution in 1789 and the Louisiana Purchase of 1803 removed or mitigated some of the most serious causes of political instability, including governmental obstructions to commerce, the sectionalism which the framers of the Constitution had sought to combat in the 1780's remained a very real problem in Jefferson's Administration. Thus, he made quite clear in his Annual Message of 1806 his conviction that the development of roads, rivers and canals was essential to the economic harmony of the Country. He urged that development of those means of transportation would open new channels of communication between the States, would eliminate lines of separation, would more closely identify their interests and would cement the Union by new and indissoluble ties.[40]

The hopes expressed by Jefferson for the development of the Nation's roads, rivers and canals began to take definite shape in 1808 when Secretary of the Treasury Albert Gallatin submitted his Report on Roads and Canals. This report was introduced shortly after the National Road was authorized and it enunciated a wide-ranging plan of internal improvements — both roads and canals — to be undertaken at Federal expense.[41] The report declared that the Federal Government could alone remove the obstacles — in particular the scarcity of capital and labor — to internal improvements. The report stated further that the Government's resources "are amply sufficient for the completion of every practicable improvement. . . . With these resources, and embracing the whole Union, it will complete on any given line all the improvements, however distant, which may be necessary to render the whole productive." After pointing out that the objects proposed were of national significance and would "diffuse and increase the national wealth in a very general way," the report concluded with the statement that, "The National Legislature alone, embracing every local interest, and superior to every local consideration, is competent to the selection of such national objects." [42]

Thus, the pattern of Federal responsibility for the improvement of the waterways of the Nation, combined with Congressional selection of the particular improvements, began to emerge in 1808.

Unfortunately, the precarious position of the United States in the international arena prevented Congress from pursuing a vigorous internal improvements program during the next few years. However, the War of 1812 with Great Britain did demonstrate the need for improved transportation facilities throughout the Nation. Consequently, once peace was restored and the Nation secure, President Madison again turned the attention of the Nation toward the problem of improving the waterways and roads of the country. In his Seventh Annual Message on December 5, 1815, Madison expressed the point of view of the Executive Branch:

> Among the means of advancing the public interest the occasion is a proper one for recalling the attention of Congress to the great importance of establishing throughout our Country the roads and canals which can best be executed under the national authority. No objects within the circle of political economy so richly repay the expense bestowed on them. There are none the utility of which is more universally ascertained and acknowledged; none do more honor to the governments whose wise and enlarged patriotism duly appreciates them. Nor is there any country which represents a field where nature invites more the art of man to complete her own work for his accommodation and benefit. These considerations are strengthened, moreover, by the political effect of these facilities for intercommunication in bringing and binding more closely together the various parts of our extended confederacy.

The Legislative Branch supported this policy of Federal responsibility for waterways improvement and three Congressional champions of Federal internal improvements—Daniel Webster of Massachusetts, John C. Calhoun of South Carolina, and Henry Clay of Kentucky—frequently voiced their support for such a program. Webster felt strongly that improvements of the Nation's roads and waterways must come from the Federal Government or in the nature of things they could not come at all.[43] During the debates on this issue in 1816-1817 session of Congress, John C. Calhoun, in expressing his support for comprehensive internal improvements, said:

Let us then bind the Republic together with a perfect system of roads and canals.[44]

The drive of the Congress to insure its authority for the appropriation of money for the development of the Nation's waterways reached an important milestone in 1818 when the House passed a resolution formally stating that the Congress had such power:

Resolved that Congress has power, under the Constitution, to appropriate money for the construction of post roads, military and other roads, and of canals, and for the improvement of water courses.[45]

Henry Clay led the fight for adoption of this resolution by the House because he believed, as did Webster, that acting separately the States would not be able to make the necessary improvements.[46] Clay and his fellow supporters of the resolution were undeterred by the fact that this power was not specifically enumerated in the Constitution. Rather, they saw the adoption of this resolution as being in the English tradition of expansion by Parliament of its rights and powers.

Once this resolution was adopted, the national internal improvements program became more vigorous and decisive, as both the Executive and Legislative branches worked to develop the natural advantages of the Nation. In 1820, Congress appropriated funds for the survey of the Mississippi and Ohio Rivers and their tributaries.[47] President James Monroe gave strong executive support to the Federal internal improvements program in his Message to Congress of May 4, 1822. There Monroe stated:

The advantages which would be derived from such improvements are incalculable. The facility which would be afforded to the transportation of the whole of the rich productions of our country to market would alone more than amply compensate for all the labor and expense attending them.[48]

Monroe went on to say:

It cannot be doubted that improvements for great national purposes would be better made by the National Government than by the governments of the several States.

Henry Clay emphasized this point in the Congress when he said:

There are some improvements emphatically national, which neither the policy, the power nor the interest of any State would induce it to accomplish, and which could only be effected by the application of the resources of the Nation. The improvement of the navigation of the Mississippi would furnish a striking example. [49]

Clay reaffirmed his position in replying to those who thought internal improvements should be left to the several States:

There are various objects in which many States are interested, which therefore require their joint co-operation and which would be neglected either for want of resources or from the difficulty of regulating their respective contributions, if not taken up by the General Government. [50]

As a result of such support for a national internal improvements program, Congress in 1824 authorized Federal public works in the first river-improvement bill and the first harbor improvement bill. [51] In 1826, Congress adopted the first of what was to be a long series of combined "rivers and harbors" bills. [52]

Support for internal—as distinguished from coastal harbor improvements—grew out of the needs of the Ohio country, for it was the agricultural surplus of that area which urgently demanded improved transport facilities and low-cost access to markets, [53] just as it was the dependence of the settlers upon water transport that prompted the inclusion of the free navigation clause in the Northwest Ordinance. Indeed, the early action of the Federal Government in assuming responsibility for harbor improvement was relied upon by spokesmen from western regions as a precedent for Federal assistance to the interior. Thus, in the debate on the bill to make certain "surveys and estimates on the subject of roads and canals," introduced in Congress in December, 1823, Representative James W. Gazlay of Ohio argued in favor of Congressional authority to build roads and canals in these terms:

On the sea, Congress had omnipotent power. They might appropriate millions of treasure and enrich the sea and the seaboard and its inhabitants, but to the land, the interior and its inhabitants they could give nothing; they had no power. Could such an argument be maintained for a single moment? [54]

President John Quincy Adams gave his full support to the national internal improvements program, which had begun to take positive shape in 1824, in his First Annual Message to Congress in 1825. In this message, Adams asked Congress to consider "the general principle" of internal improvements "in a more enlarged extent." It was Adams' view that the Federal

Government should carry out "works important to the whole . . . and to which neither the authority nor the resources of any one State can be adequate." [55] Later in his Third Annual Message on December 4, 1827, President Adams reiterated the sentiment of the founding fathers in supporting a Federal program of waterway and highway improvements. He stated that such improvements should be considered "treasures laid up from the contributions of the present age for the benefit of posterity rather than unrequited applications of the accruing revenues of the Nation." After Congress had appropriated $1,000,000 in May, 1828, for the Chesapeake and Ohio Canal, President Adams took great pleasure in turning the first shovel of earth for the canal on July 4, 1828. [56]

III. Consolidation of Free Waterways and Internal Improvements Policies

President Adams' successor, Andrew Jackson, made it eminently clear when he took office that he had no intention of changing presidential policy toward internal improvements. In his First Annual Message, December 8, 1829, Jackson affirmed that:

> Every member of the Union, in peace and in war, will be benefitted by the improvement of inland navigation and the construction of highways in the several States.

Moreover, in his Second Annual Message, December 6, 1830, Jackson expressly recognized the integral relationship between the policy of Federal responsibility for the improvement of the Nation's waterways and the policy of their free use:

> All improvements effected by the funds of the Nation for general use should be open to the enjoyment of all our fellow citizens, exempt from payment of tolls or any imposition of that character.

Contemporary Congressional attitudes were fully in accord with President Jackson's views concerning the essential elements of the waterways policy of the United States. Senator Tipton of Indiana expressed the prevailing sentiment on December 16, 1834, in this manner:

> The rivers of the United States are the common property of all citizens and everybody may navigate them without let or hinderance; and that the joint funds of the Nation should improve them cannot, in my judgment, be denied.[57]

15

IV. Evolution of Internal Improvements Program
to 1850

As a result of this Executive and Congressional support, the internal improvements program continued to expand during the 1830's. Federal appropriations for rivers and harbors improvement, which had begun in 1824, increased until 1838 and continued sporadically after that year.[58] It has been estimated that appropriations for internal improvements in general increased from an annual average of $702,000 during John Quincy Adams' administration to an average of $1,323,000 per year under Andrew Jackson.[59]

During this period of increased Federal appropriation for internal improvements, the several States also began to participate more fully in local programs either directly or through corporations chartered as private monopolies to construct and operate canals and to charge tolls on their use. The most famous of these projects, of course, was the Erie Canal constructed by the State of New York and completed on November 26, 1825.

Unfortunately, these programs were as varied as they were numerous and tended to be oriented toward purely local considerations without regard to the general pattern of the national internal improvements program. As more and more States developed their own internal improvements programs, it became increasingly difficult to agree upon and co-ordinate a national internal improvements policy. Consequently, in 1837, the national program virtually collapsed as a result of State and sectional conflicts which made concerted Congressional action impossible.[60]

The harmful effects of this collapse of the Federal internal improvements program were amplified by the inability of the States, acting separately, to provide a satisfactory substitute for the Federal program. As these State internal improvements programs were obviously based on the principle of localism, it is not surprising that State money was frequently spent on projects which were of solely neighborhood convenience,[61] and that consequently the States were unable to develop coordinated improvement programs. The State programs were further restricted by insufficient revenue from taxes and tolls to finance the desired development projects. As a result, the States were forced to borrow heavily through the sale of State bonds in domestic and foreign money markets. Since the money markets in the United States were not well developed in 1840, the States were particularly dependent on London and other foreign capitals for credit. Foreign financial leaders were gravely concerned about the limitations of State financing of local improvement projects. In 1840, Baring Brothers of London stated:

> If the old scheme of internal improvements of the Union is to be carried into effect on the vast scale and with the rapidity lately projected by means of foreign capital, a more comprehensive guarantee than that of the individual States will be required to raise so large an amount in a short time.[62]

After 1840, the rate of default on State bonds was so alarming that it became impossible for individual States to sell their bonds or pledge them for loans.[63] By 1844, $60 million worth of State bonds were in default, credit was not obtainable and the State internal improvement programs had collapsed.[64]

The severe recession in the American economy in 1837 and 1839 no doubt contributed in large measure, through decline in traffic and associated toll revenues, to the inability of the States to finance their local improvement programs and to meet the debts accrued in pursuing these policies.

Another basic defect of the State programs lay in the persistent tendency to implement these programs through corporations chartered as private monopolies to construct and operate the improvement. The Federal Government as well as the States aided these enterprises with grants of public lands and purchase of canal company stock. These concerns, however, tended to construct their facilities only where traffic was assured in sufficient volume for a profit. The insistent demands for transportation facilities to stimulate national development were not met, and pressure for greater Federal participation in internal improvement was intensified.[65]

It was during this period – 1830-40 – that the policy of public assistance to the railroads on a substantial scale had its origins. Canals and other waterway improvements for the most part received assistance by direct appropriations of funds or purchases of stock. The normal mode of State and Federal assistance to the railroads, however, was by grants of large tracts of land for rights-of-way,[66] although money grants were occasionally made.[67] Further direct assistance to the railroads in the 1830's and 1840's took the form of reduced duties on iron used in railroad construction. Between 1830 and 1843, when the duty was revived at the request of the manufacturers of railroad iron, the saving to the railroads amounted to $6,000,000.[68] That the railroad builders as well as the builders of roads and canals considered Federal and local assistance necessary is evidenced by the comments of Henry Varnum Poor, the editor of the *Railroad Journal*. Commenting on the State and Federal assistance for the construction of railroads in the 1830's and 1840's and the even greater assistance rendered in the 1850's, Poor said, "No new people can afford to construct their own railroads."[69] Also, Poor frequently distinguished between the older, established regions of the Country, where abundance of capital made aid unnecessary, and the newly developing areas, where government assistance was required.[70]

The experience of the several States with their individual improvement programs during the late 1830's and early 1840's fully confirmed the fears of such men as Madison, Calhoun, Webster, Clay and Gallatin, who felt that the States acting separately would not be able to provide adequate internal improvements programs. The method of financing through tolls by a private commercial enterprise had also demonstrated grave inadequacies for a developmental program of public improvements. The scope and scale of the task clearly called for what Henry Clay had described as "application of the resources of the Nation."

After the failure of local waterway improvement programs, President Tyler, ironically in a message of June 11, 1844, vetoing a rivers and harbors bill, stated what was to become the accepted view of internal improvement programs in the second half of the nineteenth century:

> The United States, therefore, is charged with its (the Mississippi's) improvement for the benefit of all, and the appropriation of governmental means to its improvement becomes indispensably necessary for the good of all.[71]

This was the same message, it will be recalled, in which the President had denounced tolls on river commerce as "burdensome and objectionable," thus reconfirming official recognition of the vital relationship between Federal responsibility for waterway improvements and freedom of their use. But, before this view could represent a true consensus, the argument as to whether Congress was permitted by the Constitution to use Federal funds for particular rivers and harbors improvements had to be finally settled. In 1846 and 1847 President Polk had vetoed rivers and harbors appropriations bills on the grounds that although the burdens of taxation to finance them would be general, their benefits would be local and partial. Therefore, according to Polk, the Federal Government could not undertake such expenditures.[72]

Abraham Lincoln, then the representative of the 7th District of Illinois, assumed the task of refuting Polk's argument. This he did so eloquently and effectively and with such continuing relevance that his speech remains worthy of extensive quotation:

> ... Now for the second position of the message, namely, that the burdens of improvements would be *general,* while their benefits would be *local* and *partial,* involving an obnoxious inequality. That there is some degree of truth in this position I shall not deny. No commercial object of Government patronage can be so exclusively *general,* as not to be of some peculiar local advantage; but, on the other hand, nothing is *so local* as not to be of some general advantage. The Navy, as I understand it, was established, and is maintained, at a great annual expense, partly to be ready for war, when war shall come, but partly also, and perhaps chiefly, for the protection of our commerce on the high seas. This latter object is, for all I can see, in principle, the same as internal improvements. The driving a pirate from the track of commerce on the broad ocean, and the removing a snag from its more narrow path in the Mississippi River cannot, I think, be distinguished in principle. Each is done to save life and property, and for nothing else. The Navy, then, is the most general in its benefits of all this class of objects; and yet even the Navy is of some peculiar advantage to Charleston, Baltimore, Philadelphia,

New York, and Boston, beyond what it is to the interior towns of
Illinois. The next most general object I can think of, would be improvements on the Mississippi River and its tributaries. They
touch thirteen of our States—Pennsylvania, Virginia, Kentucky,
Tennessee, Mississippi, Louisiana, Arkansas, Missouri, Illinois,
Indiana, Ohio, Wisconsin, and Iowa. Now I suppose it will not be
denied, that these thirteen States are a little more interested in
improvements on that great river than are the remaining seven-
teen. These instances of the Navy, and the Mississippi River,
show clearly that there is something of local advantage in the
most general objects. But the converse is also true. Nothing is so
local as not to be of some *general* benefit. Take, for instance, the
Illinois and Michigan Canal. Considered apart from its effects, it
is perfectly local. Every inch of it is within the State of Illinois.
That canal was first opened for business last April. In a very few
days we were all gratified to learn, among other things, that sugar
had been carried from New Orleans, through the canal, to Buffalo in New York. This sugar took this route, doubtless, because
it was cheaper than the old route. Supposing the benefit in the
reduction of the cost of carriage to be shared between seller and
buyer, the result is, that the New Orleans merchant sold his
sugar a little *dearer,* and the people of Buffalo sweetened their
coffee a little *cheaper* than before; a benefit resulting *from* the
canal, not to Illinois where the canal *is,* but to Louisiana and
New York, where it is *not.* In other transactions Illinois will, of
course, have her share, and perhaps the larger share too, in the
benefits of the Canal; but the instance of the sugar clearly shows
that the *benefits* of an improvement are by no means confined
to the particular locality of the improvement itself.

The just conclusion from all this is, that if the Nation refuses
to make improvements of the more general kind, because their
benefits may be somewhat local, a State may, for the same
reason, refuse to make an improvement of a local kind, because
its benefits may be somewhat general. A State may well say to
the Nation, 'If you will do nothing for me, I will do nothing for
you.' Thus it is seen, that if this argument of 'inequality' is sufficient anywhere, it is sufficient everywhere, and puts an end to
improvements altogether. I hope and believe, that if both the
Nation and the States would, in good faith, in their respective
spheres, do what they could in the way of improvements, what
of inequality might be produced in one place might be compen-
sated in another, and that the sum of the whole might not be very
unequal. But suppose, after all, there should be some degree of
inequality: inequality is certainly never to be embraced for its
own sake; but is every good thing to be discarded which may be
inseparably connected with some degree of it? If so, we must
discard all government. This Capitol is built at the public expense, for the public benefit; but does anyone doubt that it is of

some peculiar local advantage to the property holders and business people of Washington? Shall we remove it for this reason? And if so, where shall we set it down, and be free from the difficulty? To make sure of our object, shall we locate it nowhere? And have Congress hereafter to hold its sessions, as the loafer lodged, 'in spots about?' I make no special allusion to the present President when I say, there are few stronger cases in this world of 'burden to the many, and benefit to the few' — of 'inequality' — than the Presidency itself is by some thought to be. An honest laborer digs coal at about 70 cents a day, while the President digs abstractions at about $70 a day. The *coal* is clearly worth more than the abstractions, and yet what a monstrous inequality in the prices! Does the President, for this reason, propose to abolish the Presidency? He *does* not, and he *ought* not. The true rule, in determing to embrace or reject anything, is not whether it have *any* evil in it, but whether it have more of evil than of good. There are few things *wholly* evil or *wholly* good. Almost everything, especially of governmental policy, is an inseparable compound of the two; so that our best judgment of the preponderance between them is continually demanded. On this principle, the President, his friends, and the world generally, act on most subjects. Why not apply it, then, upon this question? Why, as to improvements, magnify the *evil,* and stoutly refuse to see any *good* in them? [73]

V. Continued Development of the Waterways Policy 1850-1887: Impact of the Railroads

After Representative Lincoln's speech in the House, the Nation again began to accept and welcome Federal internal improvements programs. This change of the national attitude regarding these policies was in substantial measure the result of the coming of the great age of railroad building at the start of the second 50 years of the nineteenth century.

The new era of national action began in 1850 with an extensive grant of Federal lands for rights-of-way to aid in the construction of a system of railroads from Mobile, Alabama, to northern Illinois. This subsidy amounted to 3,750,000 acres and it also set a precedent for subsequent grants by Congress in 1852, 1853, 1856 and 1857 which totaled 18,000,000 acres in 10 States for the aid of 45 railroads.[74] Although this was a large figure, it was small relative to the amount later to be granted to the transcontinental railroads. The total land authorized for distribution to the various transcontinental railroads was more than 116,000,000 acres.[75]

Senator Stephen A. Douglas of Illinois mapped the strategy of combining the southern project of the Mobile and Ohio with the northern project of the Illinois Central, so that the proposed improvement could offer "a continuous railroad communication from the Gulf to the extreme limit of Illinois." The supporters of the improvement accordingly based their arguments on the projected railroad's importance as "a great national thoroughfare."[76]

22

This return to reliance on the agency of the Federal Government for internal improvements resulted in part, also, from the national reaction to the failure of the State programs described above. Senator William H. Seward of New York voiced this sentiment in the Senate in 1850, when he attributed the financial difficulties of the new States to "the circumstance that it was devolved upon their governments . . . to make works of internal improvement while the resources best applicable to that object, the public lands, belonged to the Federal Government." [77]

Another important factor contributing to the revitalization of the Federal internal improvements program was the realization of both railroad builders and members of Congress that private enterprise could not be expected to finance such a vast undertaking. It was the general opinion among railroad men that no trans-continental railroad could be built "without substantial aid, either in money or lands, from the General Government." [78]

As a result of this program of massive Federal subsidies to the railroad companies, railroads became the dominant factor in the national transportation network after 1860. [79] But with the rapid development of the railroad systems a strong reaction to their dominant role in the American transportation industry soon emerged in the Legislative and Executive branches. [80] This adverse reaction resulted principally from the railroad companies' predatory, "what-the-traffic-will-bear," rate-making policies, which in many instances were designed systematically to destroy the railway's water competitors, [81] and once monopoly was established, to raise rates to exorbitant levels.

The history of the Erie Canal provides a graphic illustration.

In 1851 the New York State Legislature passed a bill to abolish the tolls which railroad companies in direct competition with the Erie Canal had previously been required to pay. The railroads then lowered their rates to levels at which a considerable portion of the freighting business yielded no profits. [82] These toll charges against the railroads were never restored. Moreover, as a result of railroad competition the State was forced to reduce tolls on canal traffic. In 1839 the average toll was $1.12 per ton; in 1850 it was $1.06; in 1860 it was $0.64 and gradually it was further reduced to $0.12 in 1882. But regardless of these reductions, in the absence of restraint upon the railroads in their competitive onslaughts against canal traffic, the waterway tonnage continued to shift to rail. By referendum, the people of New York amended the State Constitution so as to abolish all tolls on the Erie Canal system.

President Grant expressed his dissatisfaction with, and his apprehension concerning, excessive rail rates in his Annual Message to Congress, December 1, 1873. He referred to the "lack of cheap transportation" in the Nation as contributing directly to "the recent panic [of 1873] and stringency." He then went on to recommend certain appropriations for rivers and harbors improvements as "a national work of great value to the producers of the West and South in giving them cheap transportation to the seaboard and a market and to the consumers in the East in giving them cheaper food." Not only was the Government dissatisfied with the policies of the railroads, but the Nation as a whole was so thoroughly aroused by the railroads' discrimination in freight charges among localities, articles and individuals and their corresponding coercion of merchants, farmers and communities [83] that farmers at times burned their corn rather than ship it to market at the exorbitant rates charged by the railways.[84] Governor Larrabee of Iowa expressed the sentiments of the people when he said:

> The railroad corporations were in fact rapidly assuming a position which could not be tolerated. . . . They had thoroughly gotten it into their heads that they, as common carriers, were in no way bound to afford equal facilities to all, and indeed, that it was in the last degree absurd and unreasonable to expect them to do so.[85]

Congress reacted to the railroad companies' abuse of their position of mastery in the transportation industry in two ways. First, it began investigations of railway practices and introduced regulatory legislation which culminated in the Interstate Commerce Act of 1887. Second, it appropriated funds for rivers and harbors improvements so that efficient, inexpensive water transportation, competitive with the railroads, could be made available to the American people. The first legislation passed for the purpose of filling this need was the Rivers and Harbors Appropriations Act (H.R. 3822) which was signed by President Grant on August 14, 1876. With the passage of this measure, a firm Congressional effort began to restore the inland waterways to their previous vigor and competitiveness.

The most significant appropriations bills passed during this restoration period were those of 1882–the first $10,000,000 Rivers and Harbors Appropriations Bill–and of 1884. During the course of the debates on these bills and on the Interstate Commerce Act of 1887, it became clear that Congress had a two-fold purpose in adopting waterway development and rail-regulatory legislation.

The original central purpose of internal improvements programs–to unify the Country and facilitate trade and commerce–remained the primary motivating force for the waterway improvements programs. But, combined with this, there was the growing conviction of the Congress that the railroad companies had failed to meet their responsibility to the Nation. Consequently, Congress felt it was eminently necessary to provide the Nation's producers and consumers with an inexpensive alternative to monopolistic, exorbitantly-priced railway transportation. It was assumed that if an efficient competitive means of transportation were available to shippers, the railroads would have to maintain more reasonable rates. It should be emphasized, however, that by appropriating funds for waterway improvements, the Congress sought to benefit the Nation as a whole by improving transportation facilities, without, of course, intending impairment of rail transportation. Senator Conger of Michigan expressed the sense of Congress on this point during the debates on the 1882 Appropriations Bill:

> The object of the 1882 Bill making appropriations for the construction, repair and preservation of certain works on rivers and harbors and for other purposes is to improve transportation facilities, and the construction and development of canals fulfill this purpose.[86]

Although the Congress had no intention of injuring the railroad industry, it was determined to improve the waterways so that the railways could not continue to dominate the Nation's commerce. Senator Logan of Illinois expressed this determination in 1882 when he pointed out in the debates that the arguments against canals and waterway improvements were the arguments of railroad presidents and that "being a day and age of railroads, the people of this country must have something at least to have an effect and an influence upon the railroads so that they shall not be robbed at every step they go." [87]

The views expressed in the Senate were shared fully in the House as is evidenced by the speeches made by various representatives in behalf of the 1882 Appropriations Bill. Representative Page of California, the Chairman of the House Rivers and Harbors Committee, who introduced the bill to the House, stated:

> These great national highways are the only avenues by which competition can be created with the railroad transportation of the country. Congress has allowed the rivers and harbors of this Country to remain too long unimproved so that we have been absolutely in the hands of the railroad monopolies. It has been shown by testimony before our committee that wherever there is water transportation competing with the railroad routes of the country, railroad freight rates are nearly 50 percent less than where there is no competition.[88]

The House Committee on Commerce stressed, in its report on the bill, that it was prepared to recommend passage with a view solely to the improvement of navigation on the Nation's navigable streams and for the benefit of national commerce. But, the Committee did believe:

> That at no time in the history of our Government have the people so unanimously demanded of Congress liberal appropriations for rivers and harbors. . . . and that it is of infinite importance, for the protection of the public from the undue exactions of the railroad companies, that the natural highways of commerce, the rivers of the Country, shall be placed in the best condition to compete with them.[89]

In a speech in support of this bill on the floor of the House, Representative Henderson of Illinois made a detailed attack on the discriminatory rate-making policies of the railroads and demanded waterway improvements as the means of securing cheaper transportation for the people and thereby protecting them from extortion by the railroad companies.[90]

Representative Horr of Michigan expressed the general attitude of the Congress with regard to rivers and harbors appropriations in the following manner:

> Let us take into account the whole Country and make our appropriations for the benefit of the whole Country. And, hereafter, as with the mails so with the improvement of our navigable streams, let no man talk about the amount this State or that State pays, nor the amount this State or that State receives, the only question should be is the improvement needed and is it within the borders of our growing Nation? Let us cease this

bickering about the States and rise to higher, broader considerations in the investigation of these great national subjects.[91]

That these views represented the prevailing opinion of Congress is substantiated by the fact that after President Arthur vetoed the Rivers and Harbors Appropriations Bill of 1882, because he did not think that a majority of the provisions contributed to the general welfare or national defense, Congress passed this bill over the President's veto.

The Rivers and Harbors Act of 1882 marks a significant milestone in the development of national waterways policy. For it was the first Act of Congress combining appropriations for development of the Nation's waterways with a reaffirmation of the policy of freedom from tolls or other user charges. Many acts concerning particular waterways upon Federal acquisition had prohibited tolls,[92] but here for the first time Congress expressly legislated a general prohibition of tolls on all Federal waterways in these terms:

> That no tolls or operating charges whatsoever shall be levied or collected upon any vessels, boats, dredges, craft or other water craft passing through any canal or other work for the improvement of navigation belonging to the United States.[93]

The conviction of Congress that waterway improvements must be combined with a policy of free use of these waterways was emphasized by reenactment with a slight modification of the prohibition against tolls in the Rivers and Harbors Appropriations Bill of 1884. Representative Willis of Kentucky, the Chairman of this Committee which reported the bill favorably, introduced the bill to the House and submitted the Committee's report for the record. Under the topic heading "Navigation to be Free," the report stated:

> Another provision prohibits tolls or operating charges from being levied or collected upon vessels passing through any canal or other work for the improvement of navigation belonging to the United States. Operating charges under proper restrictions are to be paid by requisitions upon the Secretary of the Treasury. This is the existing law as to the Des Moines, Portland and St. Mary's canals and there seems to be no good reason for not putting all similar Government works upon the same footing. Without such a law, the failure of one rivers and harbors bill may seriously embarrass navigation.[94]

The tenor of the Congressional debates in 1884 was practically identical with that of 1882.[95] It is clear from the debates of both these years that Congress was very concerned with the need to improve the inland waterways of the Nation in order to enhance the Nation's transportation system and to provide transportation facilities cheaper than the railways. Given this concern of Congress with the task of assuring inexpensive transportation rates in order to develop commerce, tolls or user charges on canals and rivers would have been self-defeating. Consequently, Congress decided in 1884 to guard against any misunderstanding of its policy and again, as in 1882, stated categorically in the Rivers and Harbors Act [96] that navigation on the improved waterways was to be free from "tolls or operating charges."

The interest of Congress in the need to maintain inexpensive transportation in the United States took the form of action not only in the rivers and harbors appropriations bills but also in the Act to Regulate Interstate Commerce which was introduced in December, 1884, and which became law in 1887. The Congressional debates and the hearings before the cognizant Congressional Committees provide an excellent insight into the attitude of Congress about this problem. In forming this legislation Congress realized that, as Senator Conger of Michigan said, "The waterways control the railroads better than any legislation we can have. All up and down the current of these waters, they control the prices and the monopolies of the railroads."[97] Nevertheless, by means of this regulatory legislation, Congress sought to provide additional protection against the evil of predatory rate-cutting described by Senator Beck of Kentucky as:

A railroad being permitted to reduce its rates below the cost of hauling at the end of a line in order to run off some competing line or waterway, so that the railroads may absorb the trade; and the moment they run off their competitors put up the price to what they please, and in the meantime make up the loss they incur on through hauls by doubling, trebling and quadrupling the charges upon the products of the people along the line."[98]

It was generally felt that no similar regulatory legislation with respect to waterways was necessary because "the railroads have the exclusive use of their roads and this situation creates reasons for legislative action that do not exist on the waterways."[99] This attitude was summed up by Representative Reagan of Texas:

> What is the necessity of regulating the rates of transportation in commerce on the open waterways of the country – the navigable rivers, the lakes and the bays? They are now free public highways of commerce, which all may navigate who will. No person and no company has, or can have exclusive control of them, as these corporations do have exclusive control of the railroads. And so far the people have been able safely to rely on the competition between the different vessel owners who navigate the public waters for that competition, which has secured to them reasonable freight rates and freedom from unjust discrimination.[100]

The debates preceding 1887 on the Bill (H.R. 5461) which led to the Act to Regulate Commerce also point up the Congressional recognition of the incompatibility of tolls or user charges with the status of the waterways as free public highways. The following illustrative exchange occurred between the Chairman of the Senate Commerce Committee and Chauncey M. Depew, Counsel for the New York Central Railroad, during the hearing in 1884 on the Bill:

Mr. Depew said:

> The Government goes to work and establishes light-houses and buoys. It employs a large force to dig a canal at an expense of millions and millions of dollars and makes it absolutely free, and imposes a tax for the purpose of sustaining it, upon the people of the Country. A carrier goes on the railroad with his cars at New York and he is to be taxed and regulated and restricted in his charges. Another goes by the canals or rivers upon the road-bed provided by the Government, and yet he is not taxed or regulated; he is fostered and encouraged. He is not controlled and regulated, while his rival upon the lands to whom the Government contributes no guarantes and grants of privileges is bound and tied down.

The Chairman replied:

> If the railroads were managed as Mr. Sellers said the Pennsylvania Railroad was prior to 1857, that any person could put a train of cars on and run them, they would be put on a parity with the lakes; but when they have the exclusive use of their roads there are reasons for legislative action that do not exist on the waterways.

Thus, Congress was determined to prevent the railroads from using their discriminatory rate policies to force their water competitors out of business. The Nation's transportation system had been founded on the availability of vigorous, competitive water transportation and Congress was resolved to guard against the destruction of this source of cheap transportation by the railroad monopolies.[101] The Interstate Commerce Act of 1887 established the principle of Federal regulation of railroads, and created the machinery for such regulation,[102] *in conjunction with the regulatory influence of waterway competition operating under the historic policy of freedom from tolls or special taxes.*

VI. 1907-1939, Resurgence of
Waterway Development

During the 1880's and 1890's public opinion throughout the Middle West continued to gather in support of rehabilitation of internal navigation. But, development of the Nation's waterways proceeded without significant acceleration until 1907 when President Theodore Roosevelt, disappointed with the progress which had been made and concerned about the condition of the Nation's transportation system, called for more dynamic Federal action in the improvement of the Nation's natural highways.[103] On December 8, 1908, in a Special Message to the House and Senate on Inland Waterways, he demanded immediate action to achieve quicker and more impressive results from the improvements program. The President said:

> Until the work of river improvement is undertaken in a modern way, it cannot have results that will meet the needs of a modern Nation. These needs should be met without further dilly-dallying and delay. The essential thing is that the work should go forward under the best possible plan and with the least possible delay. The time for playing with our waterways is past. The Country demands results.

Congress shared the concern of the President over the inadequacy of the Nation's transportation network. Representative Ransdell of Louisiana complained that "many communities have suffered terribly because a lack of transportation facilities prevented them from moving their commodities." [104]

31

Senator Newlands of Nevada attributed the malaise of the transportation system to the inability of the railways to meet the demands of the production of the country. He explained:

> Years ago the railways were competing with the waterways and nearly drove them out of business. But the efforts of the railways to monopolize the carriage of cheap natural products, carried in other countries by water, has resulted in congestion of traffic and a virtual breaking down of the entire transportation system; and it is essential that we shall take immediate steps to supplement our railway system by a complete system of waterway transportation.[105]

With regard to the transportation industry as a whole, Senator Newlands was of the opinion that it was of the highest importance that machinery should be adjusted so that the "best and cheapest use, in the interest of the public," can be made of "all of the public highways – of river, of railway and of ocean."[106] Previous statements of members of the Legislative Branch have shown that Congress meant this type of use to involve an important contribution by the waterways. To achieve this contribution, Senator Newlands recommended that, "After these waterways are developed they must, of course, be freely used by the people."[107] This recommendation provides additional evidence that the Federal improvement of the Nation's waterways and the free use of them by the public were the essence of the national waterways policy in the mind of Congress. Clearly, also, Congress was well aware that the waterways must be protected against the destructive competition of the railways. As Senator Newlands put the matter:

> The Nation ought not to allow one public servant (the railroad company) to destroy another public servant (the waterway company), both engaged in conducting traffic on the public highways of the country.

Manifestly the improvement of the waterways would not bring about the desired beneficial effects in the Nation's economy if water carriers were to be subjected to the predatory rate-making practices of the railroad companies.[108]

Thus, the great ends of public policy which Congress during this period sought to serve by improvement of the inland waterways were (a) provision of water transportation with the capability to withstand the predatory practices of the railroads in order to assure operation of the regulatory influence of inter-carrier competition upon the railroads,[109] and (b) expansion of the availability of cheap transportation for the benefit of the economy of the Nation.[110]

Clearly, the Congress was considering the public welfare in the broadest sense. There is no indication of any interest in the water carriers, except insofar as they would be the instrument of policy. The formation of the Inland Waterways Corporation in 1918 was no exception. The stated purpose of Congress in organizing and operating the Federal Barge Lines was to "rehabilitate river transportation to further the development of less-than-barge-load traffic and a system of joint rail-barge rates which it was hoped would bring the advantages of water transportation to shippers at interior points."[111]

If, however, any particular interest spurred Congress and the Executive to improve the Nation's waterways, it was the determination to furnish the farmer with a means of cheap transportation for agricultural products. President Harding expressed his interest in this problem in an address in Kansas City, Missouri, June 22, 1923, when he said "the use of our inland waterways offers the one sure way to reduce carrying charges on basic materials, heavy cargoes, and farm products. Probably all of us acknowledge the urgent need of diminished costs on agricultural shipments and many bulk cargoes essential to the manufacturing industry."[112] Calvin Coolidge made his interest in securing cheap transportation for the farmer known as soon as he was nominated for the Presidency by stating:

> The farmer should have the benefit of legislation providing for flood control and the development of inland waterways, better navigation east and south from the Great Lakes . . . [113]

During this period, Members of Congress were stressing not only the general benefits which the improvement of internal waterways would bring to all sectors of the economy but also the benefits which would accrue to the farmer as a result of these improvements.[114] During debates on the Rivers and Harbors and Navigation Bill of 1925, Representative Kvale of Minnesota stated on the floor of the House that:

> The absorbing question for the farmers of the West is no longer one of production. . . . The question of distribution is the vital problem; it demands solution very soon. Trainloads of food are rotting on the ground merely because transportation rates are too

high to warrant their carriage to market; when rates are substantially lowered the problems of the Northwest are more than half solved. [115]

In the same vein, Representative Hull of Illinois argued that:

The farmer today is clamoring for cheap transportation, and his only opportunity, in my opinion, is to utilize the rivers of the country.[116]

Representative Lozier of Missouri vigorously emphasized the benefits to the farmer of inland waterways improvements *per se* and the benefits of cheaper rail freight rates which would result from more active competition between the waterways and the railroads. "Without this competition that exists when our inland waterways are developed," Lozier said, "the railroads would have no competition and could advance freight charges steadily." [117] He then went on to state:

When this inland waterways system is completed, the saving in freight costs each year will probably exceed the total cost incident to the improvement and development of all of our harbors and internal waterways. This expenditure will be returned every year in reduced freight rates.[118]

The point of view expressed by Presidents Harding and Coolidge was also held by President Hoover, an ardent proponent of improving the inland waterways system, who spoke out in vigorous support of these improvement projects. As Secretary of Commerce, Hoover had advocated the improvement of the inland waterways "because it will contribute to the wealth and economic progress of every section of the Union. It will contribute to the unity of the Nation. It is of concern to every one of our millions of farms and homes."[119] Hoover shared the view, expressed by Calvin Coolidge in his First Annual Message to Congress, December 6, 1923, that expenditures for waterway development are compatible with economy, as they are in the nature of capital investment. [120] As President, Hoover encouraged these "capital investments" because, as he said, "they are not local in their benefits. They are universal in promoting the prosperity of the Nation."[121]

Congress continued to share the enthusiasm of the Executive for comprehensive development of the Nation's inland navigation facilities for the national benefit. During the debates on rivers and harbors authorization and appropriations legislation in the 1930's, members of both bodies of Congress stressed in words similar to those of their predecessors the advantages to be derived by the Nation from the improvement of the internal waterways system. Thus, Representative Mansfield of Texas, the Chairman of the House Rivers and Harbors Committee, discussed this Congressional tradition and said:

Congress, during a period of more than 110 years, has established its policy on well-defined lines for continued improvement of national waterways to meet the requirements of commerce and navigation.[122]

In addition to enumerating the benefits of these improvements for the economy as a whole, Members of Congress continued to stress the particular beneficial effects of waterway improvements on the rate-making policies of the railroads. Combined with this discussion was an analysis of the basic differences between the rail and water transportation industries. Representative Colden of California, in a lengthy speech on the floor, April 8, 1935, stated this position most comprehensively:

1427627

The railways have made it increasingly difficult to develop and maintain water transportation. In some instances this obstruction has taken the form of the purchase of canals and the relegation of their use; in other instances the railways have reduced their rates between points competitive with waterways thereby making it impossible to develop any great volume of water transport. . . . Furthermore, there is a fundamental difference between railway and water transportation. The railway by its very nature is a monopoly. *Its lines or its rails are under the exclusive management of a great corporation which owns and controls the engines and cars that move on the tracks. There can be no competition with other agencies so far as the use of the railway equipment is concerned. The shipper and the public must deal upon the terms of the railway within the regulations which have been imposed upon the railways by a dissatisfied public.* (Emphasis supplied)
On the other hand water transportation . . . invites open competition and no steamship company and no barge line can monopolize the watercourse . . . River, lake and ocean – these great highways are free and open beyond the power of monopolization. It is not only the privilege but the duty of Congress to support the development of an adequate, comprehensive and co-ordinated waterway system that will serve all the people of all the country whenever and wherever the cost is economically justifiable.[123]

While recognizing the beneficial effects of improved waterway transportation with regard to railroad freight rates, Congress emphasized that the waterways should not be viewed
solely as competitors of the railroads but also as a complemen-
tary mode of transportation within an integrated national
transportation network. In this respect, Congress shared the
view of Herbert Hoover [124] that "new transportation facilities create business" and, as Hoover did, it felt that the railways could well benefit through the provision of increased
traffic by fully developed waterways. In support of this view,
Representative Culkin of New York noted that a letter from
Representative Mansfield informed him that 90 per cent of
the harbor improvements – increases of harbor depth necessi-
tated by increases in tonnage – in America were requested by
the railroads. [125] In this same speech, Representative Culkin
reminded his colleagues that:

> Sixty years ago it was the belief of German and English steel
> manufacturers that America could not compete internationally,
> because over 1500 miles separated her coal from the ore of the
> Messabi Range in Minnesota. However, with the waterways car-
> rying the ores from the Messabi Range at one-twentieth the
> cost for which the railroads would carry them, the development
> of Pittsburgh was made possible as a great steel manufacturing
> center and resultantly as one of the greatest railroad centers in
> the world. [126]

During the 1930's Congress also joined with the Administration of President Franklin D. Roosevelt in an attempt to
develop effective public works programs in order to stimulate
the national economy and bring the Nation out of the economic
depression which had gripped it since October, 1929. Congress
viewed the rivers and harbors improvement program as an
essential part of the general public works program to increase
employment. Representative Eckert of Pennsylvania, speaking
in 1935 in behalf of waterway improvements legislation, expressed succinctly the view of Congress on this point:

> Much is being said these days about the relief of the unemployed,
> of raising the American standard of living, and providing hap-
> pier conditions for the average man and woman. To bring relief
> to the unemployed is a laudable ambition on the part of the Fed-
> eral Government. To do so in the present economic crisis, the
> Federal Government is about to engage in an extensive public
> works program. Various projects are in contemplation, including
> the improvement of rivers and harbors. [127]

The Congress preferred inland waterway improvements to the other types of public works projects which were contemplated because, as Representative Eckert said, "The development of our river systems and harbors, as indicated, is not only permanently improving the economic conditions of the present generation, but of generations yet to be.''[128] Representative Colden's rhetorical question expressed his concurrence in this view:

> Is it not a fact that the money we are now expending for recovery, particularly, must be paid by future generations and that by the improvement of our rivers and harbors we are giving future generations something for the encumbrances they must pay?[129]

Furthermore, the waterway development projects provided an excellent remedy for the most pressing problem of the time: unemployment. Representative Cole of Maryland told his fellow Congressmen, "I doubt if there is any other project contemplated under the public works program which would absorb as much labor as this one [the Rivers and Harbors program of 1935]." [130]

For these reasons, as expressed by Members of Congress, the inland waterways improvements program of 1935 was approved by Congress and the Executive as a part of the emergency public works program designed to meet the economic crisis of the 1930's and as a part of the comprehensive, 115-year-old Congressional program for improving the navigation facilities of the Nation.

VII.   1940-1967, The Modern Period

During the years of World War II, the attention and efforts of the President and Congress were fully devoted to the successful prosecution of the war effort. However, President Roosevelt indicated his awareness of the importance of the inland waterway system to national defense very early in the emergency period. In a letter to Dewey Short, the president of the National Rivers and Harbors Congress, on October 27, 1941, President Roosevelt said:

> The importance of our harbors and coastal and inland waterways in strengthening the Nation's transportation system to meet the increasing demands of the defense program is conspicuously demonstrated. . . . For example, the intracoastal waterway extending along the Gulf and Atlantic coasts although not fully developed is today a potent factor in alleviating the coastwise shipping problem. Likewise the various dams and reservoirs and related works constructed in the interest of navigation, flood control, power, water conservation and other purposes are being called upon to contribute their utmost to the defense effort.

Shortly thereafter, on February 10, 1942, in a letter to Chairman Mansfield of the House Rivers and Harbors Committee, President Roosevelt re-emphasized his interest in developing the Nation's waterways to help meet the national emergency:

> I invite your attention to the need for expediting legislative action on H.R. 5993. At this time it is important that every phase of construction contributory to the Nation's armament be prosecuted with the utmost dispatch. Certain waterway improvements for navigation and power production are especially desirable for the transportation and production of war materials.

The bill in question authorizes improvements in the interest of national security and the stabilization of employment and provides that the projects authorized shall be prosecuted as speedily as may be consistent with budgetary requirements . . .

The experience of the Nation during World War II fully established the importance of the inland waterway system to national defense as well as to the national economy.[131] Consequently, in 1946, Congress began anew its efforts to improve the navigation facilities on the inland waterways, and it has enthusiastically carried out this policy up to the present time. The debates on legislation for improving the Nation's waterways during the post-war era have continued in a vein which had become familiar during the previous 125 years of Congressional waterways policy.

The tradition of Federal responsibility for the improvement of inland waterways is well understood by Members of Congress. Representative Edward A. Garmatz of Maryland reminded his colleagues in 1956 that:

The navigation system has been the responsibility of the Federal Government since the Nation was founded. The investment made in the program has resulted in substantial and widespread benefits from the standpoint of economics and national welfare.[132]

In supporting rivers and harbors authorization and appropriations legislation during the last 20 years, Congress had continued to emphasize the benefits which the national economy has always derived from low-cost water transportation. The Public Works Committee of the House stated in its report on the Rivers and Harbors Authorization Bill of 1949 that:

Since our earliest days low-cost water transportation has been an important factor in our economic well-being. The same is strikingly true today with our more complex and competitive economy.[133]

Recognizing the important role of water resource development and other public works activities as an instrument for shaping economic trends, President Eisenhower in his State of the Union Message of January 6, 1956, said:

But public works activities are closely interrelated and have a substantial influence on the growth of the Country. Moreover, in times of economic contraction, they may become a valuable sustaining force.

Similarly, Senator Richard L. Neuberger of Oregon, during the Senate debates on the Rivers and Harbors Authorization Act of 1956, declared:

> These public works programs contemplate full coordination with other related programs to produce the ultimate economic utilization and development of our water resources and will contribute materially to the economic well-being of the Nation.[134]

Representative Clifford Davis of Tennessee, as Chairman of the Flood Control Subcommittee of the House Public Works Committee, emphasized this theme in his speech in support of the Rivers and Harbors Authorization Bill of 1962. (H.R. 13273):

> The broad objectives of this program are the full efficient development, utilization and conservation of the Nation's rivers and the protection and development of its coasts as a means of advancing the national economy and enhancing the welfare of the people.[135]

During the 1962 debates, Representative Robert E. Jones of Alabama also stressed the wide range of economic benefits produced by the improvement of America's waterways:

> Our interior waterways and our coastal waterways with their associated facilities form a critical transportation complex of paramount importance to agriculture, industry and national security. It is an essential element of our national policy that our navigable water resources be developed and used to the fullest economical extent. Low-cost water transportation is a significant factor in the location and establishment of industry today — and will be in the future — as it has been in the past.[136]

At the dedication of the Barkley Lock and Dam on the Cumberland River in Kentucky in September 1966, Vice President Hubert H. Humphrey accorded full recognition to the economic stimulus provided by waterway improvements, saying:

> My, what new industries will spring up — new industries, new jobs, new wealth, new business and more pleasure and recreation . . . This development is a model for the Nation. But what we see here before us today can give us a much wider hope.[137]

In the same vein, Representative William H. Natcher of Kentucky, commenting on the importance to industrial expansion of modern navigation facilities on the Ohio River, said in August 1966:

The Ohio River is destined to be one of the chief catalysts for growth in Kentucky in the years ahead.[138]

In one of the most recent expressions of Congressional evaluation of the waterways program, the Report of the House Committee on Appropriations on the Public Works Appropriations Bill, 1967, put the matter in these terms:

The navigation system of harbors and waterways constructed by the Corps of Engineers now carries almost 1¼ billion tons of traffic annually, principally in those commercial items which do not require rapid movement but which are essential to the growing industrial economy of the Nation. Prominent among these commodities are 462 million tons (about 137 billion gallons) of petroleum and its products, 206 million tons of coal and coke, 146 million tons of iron ore, iron and steel, and 106 million tons of sand, gravel and stone. The waterways now carry annually about 250 billion ton-miles of freight traffic, continuing their increasing trend, and account for the movement of approximately one-sixth of the total ton-mileage of the Nation's intercity traffic.

At the same time, the more than 240 million acre-feet of storage space provided in nearly 300 Corps of Engineers reservoirs completed or under construction constitute a significant national resource for conserving the water and controlling the flows of our rivers to help meet the growing water supply requirements of thousands of industries and hundreds of American communities. It is estimated that from 1952 through 1965 a total of 5,882 new industrial plant projects were established in the United States on the inland river banks to obtain the increasingly important advantages of water transportation, water supply and other water uses.[139]

It is clear, therefore, that throughout the history of American waterways policy Congress has carried out its program of Federal development of inland waterways because of the vast range of benefits which this development brought to the Nation as a whole. Furthermore, it is evident that during the implementation of the Congressional program for waterways improvements, the Congress has recognized that the policy established in the 18th Century, prescribing free use of these waterways by all citizens, has been at every stage of this development program a vital element in assuring that the waterway improvements effected the desired economic benefits.

Thus, the House Public Works Committee's report recommending passage of the St. Lawrence Seaway Bill emphatically reaffirmed the domestic free waterways policy. The Committee stated:

> In approving the imposition of tolls as part of this project, the Committee wants it understood that by such action it is not digressing from the firm and long-standing toll-free policy established with respect to inland waterways. The approval herein given is not intended to be interpreted as a precedent varying the toll-free policy since this project, being international, is clearly distinguishable from purely inland waterway facilities in the United States.[140]

In a 1956 speech, Representative Homer D. Angell of Oregon praised the contribution of the Nation's rivers and canals to the national defense effort in World War II and then quoted Theodore Roosevelt to explain why Congress felt that the people should be able to use the inland waterways without charge:

> The improvement of our inland waterways can be and should be made to pay for itself as far as practicable from the incidental proceeds from water-power and other uses. *Navigation should of course be free,* but the greatest return [from these improvements] will come from the increased commerce, growth and prosperity of our people.[141] (Emphasis supplied)

Proponents of rivers and harbors improvements have generally argued that these improvements should be regarded as capital investments which will pay for themselves time and again by their contributions to the growth of the economy and the prosperity of the people. Representative Russell V. Mack of Washington reminded his colleagues of this Congressional point of view in 1959:

> These rivers and harbors projects have added to the wealth, prosperity and employment of the Nation, and through the benefits they create, have paid for themselves time and again.[142]

Representative John James Flynt, Jr., of Georgia reiterated this philosophy in 1962 when, in supporting the Rivers and Harbors Authorization Bill of that year, he said:

> The projects which are authorized by this legislation are in the nature of capital investments which will be of benefit to our Nation and its citizens for many years ahead. Most of these projects are self-liquidating, and over the period of their lives will return to the Treasury of the U.S. more than the capital outlay, including cost of construction, interest charges and maintenance of operation.[143]

In the Report (No. 29, 87th Congress, 1st Session) of the Select Committee on National Water Resources, under the Chairmanship of the late Senator Robert S. Kerr of Oklahoma, the broad scale of public benefits of Federal water resource projects was cited in support of payment of the Federal share from general tax revenues. Thus, the Report states at Page 23:

> With few exceptions, Federal work in the water resources field has been primarily in those areas where the benefits are widespread, or are intangible, so that local interests are unwilling or unable to pay the costs. Strong justification can be presented also for some Federal work on water resources as an element of our national defenses. Ideally, responsibility for bearing costs should be divided, between the Federal Government, *with its funds derived from general tax revenues,* and non-Federal interests, using funds put up by specific localities, in proportion to the national and local benefits. But the division point is not easy to determine. The committee believes that the national or nonlocal benefits should be given more stress in the reports that are presented by the various Federal agencies to the Congress recommending authorization of projects, and suggests that the Federal agencies devise methods for measurement of these benefits. Likewise, attention should be given to national defense aspects of water resources development.
>
> The committee is not overly concerned with the cost-sharing aspect of our water resources problems, because it believes that the present policies tend to even out the sharing of costs over the long run, among all the people. (Emphasis supplied)

The vigorous refusal of the Congress to permit the free waterways policy to be compromised in any way was exemplified during the 1964 House debates on H.R. 3846, a bill to establish the Land and Water Conservation Fund. By this bill, as introduced, the President was authorized to establish fees for the recreational use of bodies of water. Many Members of Congress foresaw the possible far-reaching and harmful effects of such a provision and protested strongly against it.[144] Representative Ed Edmondson of Oklahoma pointed out:

> The present language of the bill provides for fees only on recreational boats on waters that are units in a navigation system. It is my conviction that this could be a fatal wedge for waterway tolls if it were allowed to stand.[145]

In response to the protests of his colleagues and because he understood the feelings of his colleagues about navigable waters "and most certainly did not wish to upset the traditional customs that we have followed in the past as far as charges of navigable waters are concerned,"[146] Representative Wayne N. Aspinall of Colorado, the Chairman of the House Interior and Insular Affairs Committee, offered an amendment to this legislation which was agreed to by the House. This amendment provided that:

> No fee of any kind shall be charged under any provision of this act for use of waters that are in fact navigated by commercial freight-carrying vessels.[147]

The Senate adopted a further amendment eliminating all charges for the use of waters. This was concurred in by the House and now stands as part of the Land and Water Conservation Fund Act of 1965, reaffirming the long-established free waterways policy.

A critical test to determine whether the American system of toll-free waterways will be abolished or continued may occur in the near future, since the Executive Branch has proposed initiation of waterway user charges in the form of a tax on fuel used in vessels of 15-foot maximum draft or less.[148]

Concerned by rising agitation for waterway user charges within the Executive Branch, prominent Senators and Congressmen have recently spoken out in defense of established policy.

Thus, Senator Stephen M. Young of Ohio [149] has contended that "the use of the waterways of our States and the Nation should always be available and free to all our citizens." Senator John Sherman Cooper of Kentucky [150] has warned that "special charges and taxes on the use of America's historically free waterways . . . would serve only to retard essential [water resource] development." Senator Allen J. Ellender of Louisiana [151] and Representative Hale Boggs of Louisiana [152] have opposed such charges as prejudicial to water-based industries, with dislocative effects upon competitive relationships. Senator John Stennis of Mississippi [153] has predicted injury to the national economy through curtailment of business and increased inflationary pressures through higher transportation costs, as a consequence of waterway user charges. Representative Michael J. Kirwan of Ohio [154], pledging his "unalterable opposition" to waterway user charge proposals, has also stated his conviction that such charges would impede water resource development as well as industrial expansion and "would create unnecessary and hazardous inflationary pressures."

Representative William H. Harsha of Ohio [155] has denounced waterway user charges as violating the free waterways covenant of the Northwest Ordinance of 1787, as a breach of faith with those who have invested large sums along the navigable streams and as inflationary in character. Opposing tolls on the Gulf Intracoastal Waterway, Representative John Young of Texas [156] has contended that the waterway had more than paid for itself in "taxes generated . . . not to mention profits derived by producers and consumers from the availability of the best and cheapest bulk transportation in the world." Representative Wilbur D. Mills of Arkansas,[157] Chairman of the House Committee on Ways and Means, forecasting that water transportation would play "an ever increasing and vital part in the total economy of our Nation," has characterized proposals for waterway user charges as "unnecessary irritants" to the Congress and the American people. Senator Thruston B. Morton of Kentucky,[158] pointing out that our river valleys were developed because of toll-free water transportation, has warned against changing the rules in the middle of the game as involving the risk of sending the country into "an economic tail spin."

Illustrative of growing public awareness of the values of toll-free water transportation in a modern economy is the resolution [159] unanimously adopted by the Southern Governors' Conference in September 1966, recording "its opposition to waterway tolls or user charges in any form or in any amount" and recommending "firm adherence to long established national free waterways policy as an effective instrument in serving vital objectives of public policy such as economic growth, regional rehabilitation and sound development of the Nation's water resources."

Although the outcome of the waterway user charge issue is difficult to predict, it may be said that throughout the history of the Republic, Congress has regarded the Nation's waterways – open to all without toll or tax – as of vital importance to the development of the national economy and the prosperity of the people. In this settled conviction, the Congress has regularly provided for their improvement and has consistently adhered to the free navigation covenant of the Northwest Ordinance. Certainly, there has been a broad Congressional consensus that the traditional policy has served the Nation well in every phase of its development from wilderness to world power, and that it continues to play a major role in the economic well-being of the people.

It is perhaps of interest to note that when President James K. Polk in 1848 proposed internal improvement financing through tonnage duties, Abraham Lincoln's reply in the speech above quoted was as follows:

> Mr. Chairman, the President seems to think that enough may be done in the way of improvements, by means of tonnage duties, under State authority, with the consent of the General Government. Now I suppose this matter of tonnage duties is well enough in its own sphere. I suppose it may be efficient, and perhaps *sufficient*, to make slight improvements and repairs in harbors already in use and not much out of repair. But if I have any correct general idea of it, it must be wholly inefficient for any generally beneficent purposes of improvement. I know very little, or rather nothing at all, of the practical matter of levying and collecting tonnage duties; but I suppose one of its principles must be, to lay a duty, for the improvement of any particular harbor, *upon the tonnage coming into that harbor*. To do otherwise — to collect money in *one* harbor to be expended on improvements in *another* — would be an extremely aggravated form of that inequality which the President so much deprecates. If I be right in this, how could we make any entirely new improvements by means of tonnage duties? How make a road, a canal, or clear a greatly obstructed river? The idea that we could, involves the same absurdity of the Irish bull about the new boots: 'I shall niver git 'em on,' says Patrick, 'till I wear 'em a day or two, and stretch 'em a little.' We shall never make a canal by tonnage duties, until it shall already have been made awhile, so the tonnage can get into it.[160]

Lincoln's wisdom prevailed in 1848. The policy of internal improvements and freedom of use was sustained. Congress stayed on the course established by its predecessors in 1787. This course it has unswervingly maintained to this day.

Conclusion

Over the generations, the policy of toll-free waterways improved and maintained as a sovereign responsibility of the National Government has served a variety of basic public purposes: the unification of the Country, the furtherance of westward expansion, the defeat of sectionalism with its internal trade barriers and discriminatory impositions upon commerce, and the provision of low-cost transportation adequate to the needs of a growing economy – both directly and as a restraint on the rates charged by competing overland transport modes which were so exorbitant as to obstruct economic development of regions and communities.

Waterways improvement without toll or tax has been effectively applied to stimulating the economies of underdeveloped regions of the country through improved market outlets and access to raw material sources – on a broad scale to improvement of the farm economy through cheaper distribution – to the strengthening of national defense through provision for mass movement of fuels and critical materials and, in the nuclear and rocket age, through encouragement of industrial dispersion and provision of facilities for movement of rocket engines too massive for overland transport.

In a time of growing concern regarding the adequacy of future water supply, our established free waterways policy has been an essential element in multiple purpose water resource development permitting fuller and more efficient utilization of available sites and reducing the burden of public costs for flood control, water supply, conservation, recreation and other project features. With the rise of national responsibility for full employment and economic growth, established policy has served as a stimulus to industrial expansion and broadened employment opportunities, particularly effective in "depressed area" rehabilitation.

Congress has fully grasped the nature and importance of this flexible and potent instrument of national policy and has thus far vigorously adhered to it notwithstanding a growing tendency on the part of the Executive Branch in recent years to urge impairment of the historic freedom of American waterways through tolls, user charges or special taxes.

47

FOOTNOTES

[1] Dale Van Every, *Ark of Empire*, Ch. 1, (1963).

[2] 3. Channing, *History of the United States*, Ch. 15, (1912); Fiske, *The Critical Period in American History*, Ch. 4, (1888); Nevins, *The American States During and After the Revolution*, pp. 555-568 (1924); Warren, *The Making of the Constitution*, pp. 85-88 (1928); Alfred M. Kelly and Winfred A. Harbison, *The American Constitution; Its Origins and Development*, p. 105.

[3] Kelly and Harbison, *op. cit. supra*, p. 109 — In declaring void a tax by the State of Maryland on the sale of imports, the Supreme Court commented on the discriminatory taxing policies of the States during the Confederation as follows:

"From the vast inequality between the different States of the Confederacy, as to commercial advantages, few subjects were viewed with deeper interest or excited more irritation, than the manner in which the several States exercised, or seemed disposed to exercise, the power of laying duties on imports . . . *Brown* v. *Maryland,* 12 Wheat. 419, 438 (1827)

To like effect is the statement of the Court in 1870 that:

"Prior to the adoption of the Constitution the States attempted to regulate commerce and they also levied duties on imports and exports and duties of tonnage, and it was the embarrassment growing out of such regulation and conflicting obligations which mainly led to the abandonment of the Confederation and to the more perfect union under the present Constitution." *Cox* v. *Lott,* 79 U. S. 204, 214 (1870)

[4] Alexander Hamilton, *The Federalist,* No. 22, Great Books edition, p. 81. This passage was quoted with approval by Rep. Stevenson of Virginia when pointing out the advantages of the commerce power. *Annals of Congress,* 1824, p. 1274.

[5] During the debates in the Federal Convention of 1787, Mr. Gouverneur Morris of Pennsylvania stated that he felt a regulation to prevent State imposts on commerce was necessary to prevent the Atlantic States from endeavoring to tax the western States and promote their (Atlantic) interests by opposing the navigation of the Mississippi River. Mr. Charles Pinckney of South Carolina shared this concern about the discrimination among the several States with regard to commerce. *Documents on the Formation of the Union of the American States,* pp. 631-635, Government Printing Office, Washington, 1927.

The "tax uniformity" and "ports preference" clauses of the Constitution were also derived from this fear of discrimination among the States with regard to commerce. On August 25, 1787, Mr. Carroll and Mr. Martin of Maryland expressed their apprehensions, and the probable apprehensions of their constituents, that under the power of regulating trade the General Legislature might favor the ports of particular States, by requiring vessels destined to or from other States to enter and clear thereat, as vessels belonging or bound to Baltimore, to enter and clear at Norfolk, etc. Therefore, they offered the following proposition:

"The Legislature of the U.S. shall not oblige vessels belonging to citizens thereof or to foreigners, to enter or pay duties or imposts in any other State than in that to which they may be bound, or to clear out in any other than the State in which their cargoes may be laden on board; nor shall any privilege or immunity be granted to any vessels on entering or clearing out, or paying duties or imposts in one State in preference to another." (ibid., p. 619)

In conjunction with these proposals Messrs. Pinckney of South Carolina and McHenry of Maryland proposed "All duties, imposts and excises, prohibitions or restraints had or made by the Legislature of the U. S. shall be uniform and equal throughout the U. S." (ibid.)

The end result of the debates on these proposals is found in Art. I, Section 8, Par. 1 of the Constitution, which provides that:

"The Congress shall have power to lay and collect taxes, duties, imposts and excises, to pay the debts and provide for the common defense and general welfare of the United States; but all duties, imposts and excises shall be uniform throughout the United States."

and in Art. I, Section 9, Clause 6, which provides that:

"No preference shall be given by any regulation of commerce or revenue to the ports of one State over those of another; nor shall vessels bound to, or from, one State, be obliged to enter, clear, or pay duties in another."

[6] Edward S. Corwin, *The Constitution and What It Means Today*, 11th Edition, p. 44, Princeton University Press, Princeton, N.J., 1954.

[7] *Constitution*, Art. I, Section 8.

[8] *Constitution*, Art. I, Section 8, Par. 1 and Art. I, Section 9, Clause 6. See commentary for dates Aug. 25 – Aug. 31, 1787, *Documentary History of the Constitution of the United States*, Department of State, 1900. Also, *Formation of the Union, supra*, pp. 618-635.

[9] *Constitution*, Art. I, Section 10, Clause 3.

[10] *Constitution*, Art. I, Section 10, Clause 2.

[11] *Constitution*, Art. I, Section 9, Clause 5, and Art. I, Section 10, Par. 2.

[12] Henry Steele Commager, p. xi, Introduction to *Ark of Empire*, cited Note 1 *supra*.

[13] The response to the proposal of this treaty by the southern States is typified by the resolution adopted by the Virginia House of Delegates on November 29, 1786:

"Resolved, unanimously, that the free use and navigation of the western streams and rivers of this Commonwealth and of the waters leading into the sea, do of right appertain to the citizens thereof and ought to be considered as guaranteed to them by the laws of God and Nature as well as compact." *Journal of the Virginia House of Delegates,* Session 1786, pp. 66-67.

It was this controversy that moved the southern and western delegates to the Constitutional Convention of 1787 to insist upon the requirement that one-third of the Senators could veto any treaty. In this manner the southern States having western lands could prevent a treaty with Spain which would sacrifice their rights to free navigation of the Mississippi. McClendon, *Origin of the Two-Thirds Rule in Senate Action Upon Treaties,* Amer. Hist. Rev. XXXVI, pp. 768-772. See also Howard R. Smith, *Economic History of the United States,* p. 79. The question of Spanish control of the Mississippi River first arose during the negotiations over the price of Spain's assistance to the Colonies during the Revolutionary War. At that time Benjamin Franklin advised John Jay, the American envoy, that "I would rather agree with them [the Spanish] to buy at a great price the whole of their right on the Mississippi than sell a drop of its waters. A neighbor might as well ask me to sell my street door." Francis Wharton, *The Revolutionary Diplomatic Correspondence of the United States,* vol. IV, p. 75.

[14] Van Every, *op. cit. supra,* p.19.

[15] Dale Van Every, *op. cit. supra,* p. 18. A sense of the urgency of this matter of a connecting route as George Washington saw it, may be gleaned from his report to Governor Harrison of Virginia recommending the development of the Potomac-Monongahela Route from the Great Lakes and the Ohio to tidewater. Dale Van Every's treatment of this dramatic incident bears quotation here:

"The route (Potomac-Monongahela) lay largely in Pennsylvania, a companion State to which he, as a Virginian, referred as though it were a foreign country. It was a route, he wrote, 'not under our control; being subject to a power whose interest is opposed to the extension of their navigation, as it would be the inevitable means of withdrawing from Philadelphia all the trade of that part of its western territory which lyes beyond Laurel Hill.'

"Yet he considered the case for trade with the West so urgent that he could bring himself to advocate using the very disunion which he so deeply deplored as a club to compel union. There was, he did not hesitate to point out, a mounting threat which could be expected to deter Pennsylvania interference with Virginia-bound commerce. 'Any attempt of that government to restrain it,' he wrote, 'I am equally well persuaded wd. cause a separation of their territory; there being sensible men among them who have it in contemplation at this moment.' By 'sensible men' he meant the discontented settlers in that portion of Pennsylvania west of the mountains, many of whom were Virginians who had always resented Pennsylvania's jurisdiction and were therefore the more impatient with their economic disadvantages. Having thus envisioned the possibility of resorting, if necessary, to the incitement of secession in western Pennsylvania, he proceeded, as was his custom when he had reached a decision, immediately to action. He wrote Governor Ben-

jamin Harrison of Virginia proposing that Maryland and Virginia cooperate in the joint enterprise of river dredging and canal construction
indicated. To expedite consideration he himself went to Annapolis as
Virginia's representative. So pressing was his interest that he did not
even return to spend Christmas at Mount Vernon with his family. Stirred
to swift action by his advocacy, within weeks the legislatures of both
States had approved the project, and in February of 1785 the Potomac
Company was formed to undertake the improvement of the Potomac-
Monongahela-Ohio route, with or without Pennsylvania's acquiescence.

"Washington had no compunctions about this aggressive precipi-
tancy. This was, in his estimation, no moment to temporize. In his mind
the issue was the far greater question of national survival. Again and
again in 1784 in his journal and in his letters to Harrison and others he
emphasized his conviction that American retention of the West was in
the gravest doubt while at the same time it represented the one hope for
the preservation of the Union: "The Ohio River embraces this Commonwealth from its Northern almost to its Southern limits. It is now our
western boundary & lyes nearly parallel to our exterior, and thickest
settled Country . . . The Western Settlers have no other means of coming
to us but by long land transportation and unimproved Roads. A combination of circumstances make the present conjuncture more favorable
than any other to fix the trade of the Western Country to our Markets
. . . The way is plain, and the expence, comparatively speaking deserves
not a thought, so great would be the prize. The Western Inhabitants
would, I am persuaded meet us half way rather than be *driven* into the
arms of, or be in any wise dependent upon, foreigners; the consequence
of which would be, a separation, or a War. The way to avoid both, happily
for us, is easy, and dictated by our clearest interest. It is to open a wide
door, . . . before the trade may get into another channel . . . No well informed Mind need be told, that the flanks and rear of the United territory
are possessed by other powers, and formidable ones, too – nor how necessary it is to apply the cement of interest to bind all parts of it together,
by one indissoluble band – particularly the middle States with the
Country immediately back of them – for what ties let me ask, should we
have upon those people; and how entirely unconnected shod. we be with
them if the Spaniards on their right or Great Britain on their left, instead
of throwing stumbling blocks in their way as they now do; should invite
their trade and seek alliances with them? What, when they get strength,
which will be sooner than is generally imagined (from the emigration
of Foreigners who can have no predeliction for us, as well as the removal
(west) of our own Citizens) may be the consequence of their having
formed such connections and alliances; requires no uncommon fore-
sight to predict. The Western Settlers – from my own observation – stand
as it were on a pivot – the touch of a feather would turn them away.'

"Washington had devoted all of the first years of his public life to
opening the first way west. He was now at fifty-two embarked upon an
even more dedicated devotion of all of his last years to holding the West.
But no other Easterner realized as clearly as did he that all depended on

what he had termed 'the temper and disposition' of the Westerners themselves. During the years immediately following 1784 every conceivable circumstance was to conspire to break the tenuous bonds linking them to the infant new Nation." (*Ark of Empire* pp. 19-22)

[16] Paul M. Ogilvie, *International Waterways*, p. 274, Macmillan Co., New York, 1920.

[17] *ibid.*

[18] Van Every, *op. cit. supra*, p. 171.

[19] Van Every, *op. cit. supra*, p. 173.

[20] Van Every, *op. cit. supra*, pp. 170-175.

[21] William and Julia Cutler, *The Life of the Reverend Manasseh Cutler*, pp. 358-359.

[22] MS. in the Pickering Papers of the Massachusetts Historical Society collection. In this letter, Col. Pickering also manifested his desire that the commercial history of the European rivers not be repeated on the rivers of the United States when he wrote, "I hope we shall have no Scheldts in that Country." This was an allusion to the Scheldt River in Belgium which flows through Antwerp on its way to the sea. By the Treaty of Munster, 1648, Holland obtained the right to close navigation and after that the Dutch were able to disrupt commercial traffic on the Scheldt much to Antwerp's commercial detriment.
Col. Pickering proved to be a prophet as well as a historian because in 1839 Holland established so onerous a toll on the river that the trade of Antwerp was destroyed. It was not until 1863 that Belgium was able to repurchase Holland's right to close navigation on the Scheldt. Thereafter, navigation of the Scheldt was declared to be free. 20 *Encyclopedia Britannica*, p. 63, (1952).

[23] William and Julia Cutler, *The Life of the Reverend Manasseh Cutler*, pp. 358-359.

[24] H. S. Commager, *Documents of American History*, p. 131, 7th Ed., Appleton-Century-Crofts, 1963. 1939 *Wisconsin Law Review*, p. 551, (July 1939). Under the early decisions of the courts, the navigation clause had been regarded as fully operative and binding upon states carved out of the Territory. Thus, in *Spooner* v. *McConnell*, 1 McLean 337, 22 Fed. Cas. 934, (Cir. Ct. Dist., Ohio, 1838) in speaking of the navigation clause the Court quoted with approval from the opinion of the Supreme Court of Ohio as follows:

"This portion of the Ordinance of 1787 is as much obligatory upon the State of Ohio as our Constitution. In truth it is more so; for the Constitution may be altered by the people of the State, while this cannot be altered without the assent both of the people of the State and of the United States, through their representatives. It is an article of compact and until we assume the principle that the sovereign power of the State is not bound by compact, this clause must be considered obligatory."

Similarly, in *Jolly* v. *Terre Haute Drawbridge Co.*, 6 McLean 237 (Cir. Ct. Dist., Ohio, 1853) the Court said:

"While it is admitted that some of the articles of the compact in the Ordinance of 1787 have been superseded by the admission of the States within the Northwestern Territory into the Federal Union, it has been held by repeated judicial decisions, that the solemn guaranty (of free navigation) referred to is still in force, and is a perpetual inhibition to such States from authorizing any impediments or obstructions to the free navigation of the watercourses within its scope."

The matter was well summarized in the case of *Leverich* v. *City of Mobile* 110 Fed. 170 (Cir. Ct. S. Dist., Ala., 1867) where the Court stated the law as follows:

"It is fundamental law throughout the United States that all navigable waters are common highways, forever free to the use of all citizens of the United States without any tax, impost or duty therefor."

Certain language of the case of *Huse* v. *Glover*, 119 U.S. 543 (1886), and in the similar case *Sands* v. *Manistee River Co.*, 128 U.S. 288 (1887), has raised questions as to the continuing effect of the navigation clause of the Ordinance. In the former, the State of Illinois sought to collect tolls for passage of vessels through certain locks constructed at State expense on the Illinois River. The defendant challenged the legality of the tolls under Article IV of the Northwest Ordinance and as a tax on tonnage violating Article I, Section 10 of the U.S. Constitution.

The Supreme Court advanced three grounds for its decision upholding the legality of the tolls with respect to the Northwest Ordinance:

(1) That the Northwest Ordinance ceased to be operative upon the State of Illinois after it became a State.

(2) That "the provision of the clause that the navigable streams should be highways without any tax, impost, or duty has reference to their navigation in their natural state," and

(3) That "by the terms tax, impost, and duty, mentioned in the Ordinance is meant a charge for the use of the Government, not compensation for improvements."

This case is without weight as authority for the contention that a *Federal tax* on navigation – or the equivalent in the form of a tax on vessel fuel – is not in conflict with the Ordinance of 1787. This is not to say that Congress is without power to repeal the Ordinance; but it does mean that such a tax would be in direct violation of the covenant. A question of honor, if not of law, is involved.

First, it must be noted that the Supreme Court in *Huse* v. *Glover* was mistaken in its conclusion that the navigation clause of the Northwest Ordinance, having become a Federal statute by the Act of August 7, 1789, ceased to be operative as to any State of the old Northwest Territory upon its admission to the Union. This error was corrected by the court itself in the case of *Economy Light and Power Co.* v. *United States*, 256 U.S. 113, 65 L. Ed. 847, at p. 854 (1929), where it is stated:

"So far as the Ordinance of July 13, 1787 for the government of the Northwest Territory established public rights of highway in navigable waters capable of bearing commerce from State to State, it did not regulate internal affairs alone and was no more capable of repeal by one of the States than any other regulation of interstate commerce enacted by Congress."

Second, the attempt by the court to restrict the scope of the Ordinance to navigation of streams in their natural state (i.e., unimproved waterways), involves a broad generalization unsupported by authority and unnecessary to decision on the facts of the case. Consistent application of this interpretation would have meant that, once any navigation improvement such as removal of an obstruction was made on any stream within the scope of the Ordinance, any State having jurisdiction or the Federal Government could freely tax navigation on that stream without regard to use of or benefit to the taxpayer from such improvement. Such an interpretation would have nullified the Navigation Clause. Moreover, the court itself makes clear that its decision has to do only with "compensation for the use of artificial facilities" — not taxation of navigation without regard to the use of particular facilities.

Third, the Federal Government has no property rights in the waterways as such. *James* v. *Dravo Contracting Co.,* 302, U.S. 134 (1937). Nor do navigation improvements vest the Federal Government with property rights in the waterways, as distinguished from particular facilities, such as locks and dams which do become the property of the United States when constructed or acquired by it. See *James* v. *Dravo Contracting Co., supra.* Without a proprietary interest no "toll" can be charged. Only under its taxing power can the United States impose charges unrelated to the use of particular improvements provided or owned by it. Such taxes, as distinguished from proprietary tolls are within the literal terms of the prohibition of the Northwest Ordinance. Any such tax therefore, involves a repudiation of the Ordinance, particularly where the tax is unrelated to use and cost of, or benefits from, particular improvements.

The *Huse* and *Sands* cases must therefore be regarded as strictly limited to their precise facts: *A state or other proprietor* may charge a *toll* for the use of facilities owned in amounts related to the cost of the facilities or reasonably approximated thereto, without violation of the Northwest Ordinance or the Constitution. But State or municipal license fees not exacted as a toll or as compensation for any specific waterway improvement will be stricken down. See *Harman* v. *Chicago,* 147 U.S. 396, 37 L. Ed. 216 (1893). By operation of other Federal statutes, however, such as the Rivers and Harbors Act of June 13, 1902, Sec. 1, (32 Stat. 341) the charging of tolls by such non-Federal interests may be prohibited. All Federal tolls, of course, are forbidden by 33 USCA, Sec. 5.

No interpretation of the cases permitting States or State-authorized corporations to charge tolls for use of particular improvements owned by them can justify, as permitted by the Ordinance, a Federal tax applying generally to navigation, particularly where the tax is unrelated to use of or benefit from particular improvements. With only insignificant exceptions, Congress has steadfastly prohibited Federal tolls or operating charges on domestic waterways maintained by the Federal Government. See 33 USCA, Section 5.

25 I Stat. at Large 50-53.

26 1939 *Wisconsin Law Review*, p. 551 (July 1939).

27 Those States whose constitutions incorporated the language of Article IV of the Compact of the Ordinance of 1787 are: *Alabama*, I:24; *Alaska*, VIII:13; *California*, IX:2; *Minnesota*, II:2; *Mississippi*, IV:81; *Missouri*, I:1; *Tennessee*, I:29; and *Wisconsin*, IX:1.

28 The Congressional enabling acts or acts of admission for the following States reaffirmed the language of Article IV: *Alabama*, Enabling Act, March 2, 1819 (3 Stat. 492 Sec. 6); *California*, Act of Admission, September 9, 1850 (9 Stat. 452 Sec. 3); *Illinois*, Enabling Act, April 18, 1818 (3 Stat. 428-431); *Indiana*, Enabling Act, April 19, 1816 (3 Stat. 289-291); *Iowa*, Act of Admission, March 3, 1845 (5 Stat. 743 Sec. 3); *Louisiana*, Enabling Act, February 20, 1811 (2 Stat. 642 Sec. 3) and Act of Admission, April 8, 1812 (2 Stat, 703 Sec. 1); *Minnesota*, Enabling Act, February 26, 1857 (11 Stat. 166 Sec. 2); *Mississippi*, Enabling Act, March 1, 1817 (3 Stat. 349 Sec. 4); *Missouri*, Enabling Act, March 6, 1820 (3 Stat. 546 Sec. 2); *Ohio*, Enabling Act, April 30, 1802 (2 Stat. 174 Sec. 5); *Oregon*, Act of Admission, February 14, 1859 (11 Stat. 383 Sec. 2); and *Wisconsin*, Enabling Act, August 6, 1846 (9 Stat. 57 Sec. 3).

29 35 *Harvard Law Review*, p. 154 (1921). 2 Stat. at L. 229, 235.

30 Frederick Jackson Turner, *The Frontier in American History*, p. 187; Henry Holt and Co., N.Y. 1927.

31 Samuel E. Morison and Henry Steele Commager, *The Growth of the American Republic*, Vol. I, p. 380, N.Y., Oxford Univ. Press (1962).

The rise of trade on the Mississippi River system to New Orleans "awoke the western people to appreciation of the need for free navigation of the western waters. Early in 1803, when the future of this important waterway seemed to be so uncertain, the local newspapers in the old Northwest printed in full, with editorial comments, the debates in Congress upon the closing of the Mississippi. A petition circulated about the same time called for immediate action, with a hint that otherwise the inhabitants of the western country might be compelled to adopt measures which would result in consequences unfavorable to the harmony of the Union." Beverly W. Bond, Jr., *The Civilization of the Old Northwest*, p. 360, New York, Macmillan Co., 1934.

32 Turner, *op. cit.*, pp. 188, 189. As Turner described the sequel, "After the War of 1812 the steamboat revolutionized the transportation facilities of the Mississippi Valley . . . the great river and its affluents became the highway of a commerce that reached the West Indies, the Atlantic Coast, Europe and South America. The Mississippi Valley was an industrial entity, from Pittsburgh and Sante Fe to New Orleans. It became the most important influence in American politics and industry." (Turner, *op. cit.*, pp. 194-195)

33 Howard R. Smith, *Economic History of the United States* (Ronald, 1955), p. 103. The impact of this purchase on the Nation's waterway system was fully appreciated by the people of that time. After the purchase of Louisiana, the Ohio Assembly passed a resolution that strongly commended this acquisition of territory as a measure that had secured to the western country

the free and uncontrolled navigation of the Mississippi. (Bond, *Civilization of the Old Northwest*, p. 361).

[34] Goodrich, Carter, *Government Promotion of American Canals and Railroads 1800-1890*, p. 3, Columbia University Press, New York, 1960. Washington's interest in internal improvements was expressed on many occasions. In particular he declared this interest to the Marquis de Chastellux in a letter in 1783:

> "Prompted by these actual observations, I could not help taking a more contemplative and extensive view of the vast inland navigation of these United States and could not but be struck with the immense diffusion and importance of it; and with the goodness of that Providence which has dealt his favours to us with so profuse a hand. Would to God we may have wisdom enough to improve them." Marshall, *The Life of George Washington*, p. 65, ed. by J. Crissy, Philadelphia, 1850.

[35] James Madison, *The Federalist*, No. 42, Great Books Edition, p. 139.

[36] James Madison, *op. cit.*, No. 14, p. 61.

[37] John Jay felt that the rivers of the United States presented the States with highways for the easy communication of friendly aids and the mutual transportation and exchange of their various commodities. John Jay, *The Federalist*, No. 2, p. 31.

Alexander Hamilton stressed a theme of commercial unity through governmental unity. He believed that active commerce, extensive navigation and a flourishing marine would be the offspring of a vigorous national government. Alexander Hamilton, *op. cit.*, No. 11, p. 54.

[38] *The Reports of Alexander Hamilton: The Report on Manufactures*, pp. 178, 179, Harper and Row, N.Y., 1964.

[39] 1 Report of the President's Commission on Water Resources Policy (1950) p. 431.

[40] The Annual Message of Thomas Jefferson, December 2, 1806. Even though Jefferson denied the Constitutional power of Congress in the field of internal improvements and urged amendments to provide the necessary authority, in one major case, that of the National Road, the Federal Government had already assumed authority for internal improvements. In March 1806, Congress adopted an Act to Regulate the Laying Out and Making a Road from Cumberland in the State of Maryland. "This authorized the President to appoint commissioners for laying out the road, to determine its location after receiving their report, and to request the necessary consent from the States concerned." Goodrich, *op. cit.*, pp. 24, 25; *Annals of Congress*, 8th Congress, 1st Session, p. 851.

[41] Howard R. Smith, *op. cit.*, p. 103.

[42] Quotations from Gallatin's Report on Roads and Canals appear in Goodrich, *op. cit.*, pp. 28-32.

[43] Daniel Webster, *The Writings and Speeches of Daniel Webster*, National ed., Little, Brown and Co., Boston, 1903.

[44] *Annals of Congress*, 14th Congress, 2d Session, pp. 851-54.

[45] *Annals of Congress*, 15th Congress, 1st Session, pp. 1382-1384.

⁴⁶ Clay made his view quite clear when he said, ". . . The aggregate benefit resulting to the whole society, from a public improvement, may be such as to amply justify the investment capital in its execution, and yet that benefit may be so distributed among different and distant persons, that they can never be got to act in concert." *Henry Clay, Life and Works,* Colton edition, 1864, Vol. V, p. 115.

⁴⁷ 3 Stat. 562, 563.

⁴⁸ Also of primary importance for Monroe was the extent to which these improvements would facilitate the transportation of the Nation's army in time of war. Monroe also pointed out that this was an area which, the War of 1812 had demonstrated, needed a great deal of improvement.

⁴⁹ *Annals of Congress,* 1824, Pt. I, p. 1023.

⁵⁰ Calvin Colton, *The Works of Henry Clay,* p. 445, N.Y., 1897.

⁵¹ Act of May 24, 1824, 4 Stat. 32.

⁵² Goodrich, *op. cit.,* p. 40.

⁵³ Turner, *op. cit.,* p. 121.

⁵⁴ Quoted 1 Crosskey, *Politics and the Constitution of the United States,* p. 242 (1953).

⁵⁵ James D. Richardson, *A Compilation of the Messages and Papers of the Presidents,* Vol. II, pp. 305-316, Washington, 1909.

⁵⁶ Louis Harty, *Economic Policy and Democratic Thought,* Pennsylvania, 1776-1860, p. 92, Cambridge, Harvard University Press, 1948.

⁵⁷ *The Congressional Globe,* December 16, 1834. In supporting an appropriation for the improvement of the Wabash River, Senator Tipton pointed out that the Wabash had been made a reserved public highway by a compact between the United States and the Commonwealth of Virginia at the time of cession and also by Article IV of the Ordinance of July 13, 1787. Senator Tipton then expressed his respect for the Ordinance of 1787 by pointing out that this ordinance of Congress, which was older than the Constitution, was now embraced in the Statutes of the United States.

⁵⁸ Goodrich, op. cit., p. 42, and footnote 46, p. 305.

⁵⁹ George Taylor, *The Transportation Revolution 1815-1860,* p. 21, Rinehart, N.Y., 1951.

⁶⁰ Goodrich, *op. cit.,* pp. 45, 47; Taylor, *op. cit.,* p. 21.

⁶¹ Goodrich, *op. cit.,* p. 98.

⁶² Harvey Segal, *Cycles of Canal Construction,* p. 201, Unpublished Dissertation, Columbia 1956.

⁶³ *ibid.*

⁶⁴ Goodrich, *op. cit.,* Chapter 3, *passim.*

⁶⁵ Howard Smith, *op. cit., supra,* pp. 103-4.

⁶⁶ Goodrich, *op. cit.,* pp. 13, 14, 170. "States and Nation alike granted almost as a matter of course free right of way through public lands often with the privilege of taking timber and stone from neighboring property."

⁶⁷ Taylor, *op. cit.,* p. 94. Many early railroad surveys were made by Federal

engineers at Government expense under a law passed in 1824 and repealed in 1838. 4 U.S. Stats. at L. p. 22; 5 U.S. Stats. at L. p. 260.

[68] Taylor, *op. cit.*, p. 95. Furthermore, "from 1830 until 1841, after an agitation begun by and on behalf of the Baltimore and Ohio, they (the railroads) were given either full or partial rebates on the duties on iron imported for rails." Goodrich, *op. cit.*, p. 169.

[69] Goodrich, *op. cit.*, p. 169.

[70] *American Railroad Journal*, Vol. XXXIII (1860), p. 100; Vol. XXV (1852), p. 26; and Vol. XXVIII (1855), pp. 281, 353, 514, 609-10, 673.

[71] It should be noted that Tyler vetoed the bill because he felt certain projects had not been properly surveyed; not because he opposed the principle of rivers and harbors improvements at Federal expense.

[72] Veto Message of December 15, 1847.

[73] *Congressional Globe*, June 20, 1848. Although there was a dispute between the Executive and Congress in 1848 over the Constitutional power of the Congress to appropriate money for rivers and harbors improvements, the contemporary Treaty of Guadelupe-Hildago which became effective in 1848 between the United States and Mexico (9 Stat. 922; I Malloy 1111) with the approval of the President and the Senate, guaranteed the free navigation of the Rio Grande River to the citizens of both countries, thus exemplifying the traditional American conviction that the waterways should be free of tolls. Article VII of the Treaty specified that:

"Nor shall any tax or contribution, under any denomination or title be levied upon vessels or persons navigating the same, or upon merchandise or effects transported thereon, except in the use of landing upon one of their shores. If for the purpose of making the said rivers navigable, or for maintaining them in such state, it should be necessary or advantageous to establish any tax or contribution, this shall not be done without the consent of both Governments."

The vitality of Article VII of the Treaty of Guadelupe-Hildago was confirmed in the Gadsen Treaty of 1853 (I Malloy 1123) and in later treaties between the United States and Mexico, such as the Boundary Convention of 1884, (I Malloy 1159) and the Convention of 1944 (59 Stat. 1219).

[74] Thomas Donaldson, *The Public Domain*, House Miscellaneous Document 45, Pt. 4, 47th Congress, 2nd Session, pp. 274-277, Washington, Government Printing Office, 1884.

[75] Lewis H. Haney, *A Congressional History of Railroads in the U.S. From 1850 to 1887*, pp. 19-22, Bulletin of University of Wisconsin, No. 342, Madison, 1910.

The enactment of the Pacific Railway Acts of 1862 and 1864 enabled the Federal Government to make the grants directly to the railroad companies rather than to the States for retransfer to the companies as had previously been necessary. (Morison and Commager, *The Growth of the American Republic*, Vol. II, p. 173)

[76] Goodrich, *op. cit.*, p. 171.

[77] *Congressional Globe*, 31st Congress, 1st Session, pp. 845, 848, 851, 869, 1437.

Although the Federal Government made by far the largest grants to the railroads, the States also contributed to the rapid growth of the railroad network (1) by incorporating liberal provisions in railroad charters, (2) by actually building railroads, and (3) by supplying needed money and credit for private construction (Taylor, *op. cit.*, p. 88). Similarly, the Federal Government provided millions of dollars of credit during the railroad building era (Goodrich, *op. cit.*, p. 6).

[78] *American Railroad Journal*, Vol. XXX, p. 25 (1857).

In the House debates on the Pacific Railway Act of 1862, one Representative said, "There is no corporation or body of men or interest which will furnish any considerable portion of the outlay. We deceive ourselves if we think to get any amount worth reckoning out of private individuals." *Congressional Globe*, 37th Congress, 2nd Session, p. 1707.

[79] Taylor, *op. cit.*, pp. 164-165:

"Before 1840 the amount of traffic carried by American railways was negligible as compared with that moving on all inland waterways. By 1860 the total volume carried by the two methods was probably about equal, and the value of goods transported by railroad greatly exceeded that carried on the internal waterways."

[80] For an excellent discussion of the harmful effects of government aids to the railroad companies for construction purposes, see Goodrich, *op. cit.*, Chapter 5, particularly pages 199, 200, where commenting on the advance to the railroad companies of some $60,000,000 in bonds, he says, inter alia:

"It is, however, by no means clear that this particular price had to be paid, or that the means employed were essential to the results obtained. They served to get the roads built by private management, but they did so at heavy social costs. Small groups of insiders venturing very little capital of their own were able to build the roads with the money of the bondholders and the government, and to pay themselves quick and extraordinary returns out of the profits of construction. In the case of the Union Pacific, they were able to take out large gains even before construction was completed. In that of Central Pacific, a group of four men who had put up even less of their own money remained in sole control of a great railroad. As a result, both companies were left with greatly inflated capitalizations, which reduced their ability to provide efficient service at reasonable rates. Nor can a judgment rest on economic factors alone without taking account of the effect on the national life of the notorious evasion of the law in financing of construction and the flagrant use of financial means to secure influence in Congress."

See also Morison and Commager, *Growth of the American Republic*, Vol. II, pp. 176-184.

[81] Smith, *Economic History of the United States*, pp. 370, 474.

[82] *Annual Report of State Engineer and Surveyor*, New York Senate Document 35, 78th Session, 1855.

For a recent discussion of the collapse of State toll schedules for canals under the pressure of predatory railroad rate-cutting, see the article by Harry N. Scheiber, *The Rate-Making Power of the State in the Canal Era: A Case Study,* LXXVII, Political Science Quarterly, p. 397, September, 1962.

[83] Report of the U.S. Pacific Railway Commission (1887), Vol. I, p. 141.

[84] Morison and Commager, *op. cit.,* p. 176.

[85] Quoted in Morison and Commager, *op. cit.,* pp. 179, 180.

The railroad presidents confirmed the public's opinion of them through their words and deeds. Commenting on the attempts of government to prohibit discrimination by the railroads, Leland Stanford of the Central Pacific told his stockholders in 1878:

"There is no foundation in good reason for the attempts made by the General Government and by the States to especially control your affairs. It is a question of might, and it is to your interest to have it determined where the power resides." Morison and Commager, *op. cit.,* pp. 178, 179.

[86] *Congressional Record,* 47th Congress, 1st Session, p. 5684 (1882).

[87] *id.,* p. 5719.

Senator Logan extended his remarks to the effect that he believed in railroads as strongly as anyone, but he wanted them conducted so as to treat the people fairly. Furthermore, he felt that the only way to induce the railroads to do exactly what was right with the people was to show them that there was something else that could carry the products of the country in addition to the railroads. "Give us an opening to the seaboards," he argued, "Give us a waterway from the West to the seaboard and our farmers throughout the Country will have a profit to put in their pockets as well as the great corporations of the Country." (*id.,* pp. 5719-20)

Senator Windom of Minnesota, among others, shared this view that water transportation in competition with the railroads would have a very beneficial effect on the Nation's commerce. (*id.,* p. 5722)

[88] *Congressional Record,* 47th Congress, 1st Session, p. 4940 (1882).

[89] 47th Congress, 1st Session, House Report 1263, 1882.

[90] *Congressional Record,* 47th Congress, 1st Session, p. 4965 (1882).

Representative Henderson supported an appropriation for the projected Hennepin Canal and to this end he discussed the lack of traffic on the Illinois-Michigan Canal which he attributed to the artificially low rates charged by competing railroads.

"I have said that the railroad running along the line of a canal and the river charges the same rates – 2¾ cents per bushel – that the canal does, while the railroads off the canal for the same distances from Henry to Chicago, 130 miles, charge 7¾ cents per bushel and for the same distance from LaSalle to Chicago, 100 miles, they charge 6.6 cents per bushel. The report made by Senator Windom's committee in 1874 showed that the charges on the Chicago, Rock Island and Pacific Railroad which runs along the 100 mile length of the canal were only 53 percent of the charges on four other lines running out of Chicago for the same distance, 100 miles. Certainly nothing can show more clearly the utility of this canal and that it should be maintained in the interests of the people. Even if it did not do the business, it did secure cheaper transportation for the people.

"The Hennepin Canal, 65 miles in length, will connect the lakes with the navigable waters of the upper Mississippi and give to the Northwest cheap water transportation to the Atlantic seaboard and to the markets of our Country. The benefit of such a water connection to the people of the East as well as to the West cannot be overestimated. It is in the interests of the people. It will do more to secure cheap transportation to the people than all the legislative restrictions which could be enacted by Congress to prevent railway extortion.

"We all know what the cheap water line from Chicago to the Atlantic seaboard does in securing cheap transportation. This water line not only carries cheaply, but it compels all the railroads running from the West to the Atlantic seaboard to carry at more reasonable rates and, in that way saves annually millions of dollars to producers and consumers. . . . The truth is well known that railroads when under the competition of cheaper water transportation are invariably reasonable upon their charges, and, I am sorry to say, when not under such competition they are not. I am not unfriendly to railroads. But, when they make their freight charges so high that their stock is at a premium of 30, 40 and sometimes 60 percent and that too watered so as to double and sometimes triple the actual cost of construction and to pay such large dividends; when they claim the right to impose just such burdens upon the commerce of the Country as they think proper, to tax by way of freight rates all the products of the industry of the Country carried over their roads, then I have no sympathy to express for them and no fear of interfering with such individual enterprises. On the contrary, I believe it is the duty of the representatives of the people to take all lawful and constitutional steps to prevent extortion, to secure to the people cheaper transportation. One of the best means of doing this is to improve and construct water lines of transportation when the importance of the work is such as to justify it."

[91] *id.*, p. 4943

[92] See Note 96, below.

[93] 22 Stat. 209; 33 USCA Section 5. It appears that this was the last session of Congress in which the constitutionality of internal improvements was seriously debated. It is now well settled by the Supreme Court in such cases as *Jackson* v. *United States*, 230 U.S. 1 (1913); *Ashwander* v. *Tennessee Valley Authority*, 297 U.S. 288 (1936); *Oklahoma* v. *Atkinson*, 313 U.S. 508 (1941); and *United States* v. *Gerlach Live Stock Co.*, 339 U.S. 725 (1950) that Congress has plenary power to improve the navigable waters of the United States for public purposes.

[94] *Congressional Record*, 48th Congress, 1st Session, p. 4917 (1884).

[95] In particular, Representative Neece of Illinois pointed out that these improvements were not designed to destroy or injure the railroads but to prevent extortion by them and by developing the resources of the West and North-

west ultimately to benefit the railroads. (*id.*, p. 4928). His colleague, Representative Murphy of Iowa, also pointed out the benefits of cheap water transportation at some length. (*id.*, p. 4929.)

[96] 23 Stat. 147. Of further significance in this regard has been the policy of the Federal Government of terminating the collection of tolls upon the transfer of a non-Federal navigation facility to Federal control. The Federal Government followed this policy of immediate abolition of tolls when it took over the St. Mary's Falls Canal (21 Stat. 189, 190); privately owned improvements on the lower Monongahela River (29 Stat. 219); Cape Fear River from Wilmington to Fayetteville, North Carolina (21 Stat. at L. 475); Upper Monongahela River, Pennsylvania and West Virginia (24 Stat. at L. 318); Black River, North Carolina (24 Stat. at L. 320); Mouth of Brazos River, Texas (30 Stat. at L. 1141); Puget Sound–Lake Washington Canal, Washington (34 Stat. at L. 1108). The United States in many instances specifically prohibited tolls on facilities that were Federal from the outset: Michigan City Harbor, Indiana (14 Stat. 73, 421-62); Des Moines Rapids Canal, Mississippi River, Iowa (14 Stat. 420); Meekers Island Lock and Dam, Mississippi River, Minnesota (15 Stat. 169, 17 Stat. 562); Galena Harbor and River, Illinois (26 Stat. 448-9); specifically prohibited tolls on non-Federal facilities improved with Federal funds but remaining under non-Federal ownership: Aransas Pass and Bay, Texas (20 Stat. 371-72, 26 Stat. 105-6, 28 Stat. 26-27, 30 Stat. 1128); Little Kanawha River, West Virginia (21 Stat. 475, 22 Stat. 199, 23 Stat. 139, 24 Stat. 319, 25 Stat. 410, 26 Stat. 440); Galveston Bay, Texas (23 Stat. 135, 26 Stat. 456); St. Lawrence River, New York (32 Stat. 456); and specifically prohibited tolls on non-Federal facilities to which the United States did not contribute: Mississippi River at Grand Rapids, Minnesota (23 Stat. 154); Corpus Christi and Padre Island Harbor, Texas (26 Stat. 740-1, 27 Stat. 422, 30 Stat. 1128, 32 Stat. 341); Canal from St. Lawrence River to Massena, New York (30 Stat. 904); Channels along the New Jersey Coast (34 Stat. 800); and many others. Present law forbids tolls on all improvements by non-Federal interests. See 33 USCA, Section 565.

There appear to be only two exceptions (of short duration) to this general policy. After officially taking over the Louisville and Portland Canals in 1874, the Federal Government collected $400,000 in tolls for the operation and maintenance of the canals before the Act of May 18, 1880 (21 Stat. at p. 141) provided that these canals be toll-free with operation and maintenance costs to be paid by the Treasury. Also, after purchasing the Fox and Wisconsin Rivers improvement in 1870 the United States collected tolls for its use until the Rivers and Harbors Act of 1882 (22 Stat. at p. 209) which, with its provision for a general prohibition of tolls for all navigation improvements owned by the United States, ended the collection of tolls for the use of this improvement.

[97] Unah H. Painter, *Debate in 48th Congress 2nd Session on Interstate Commerce*, Vol. I., p. 399, Washington, 1884. Senators Van Wych of Nebraska (*id.*, p. 157), McPherson of New Jersey (Vol. 2, p. 383 (1887)), Gorman of Maryland (Vol. 2, p. 109), and Representatives Glascock of California (Vol. I, p. 221), Budd of California (*id.*, p. 109), and Woodward of Wisconsin (*id.*, 251) among others shared Senator Conger's view.

[98] *id.*, p. 241.

[99] *Arguments and Statements before the Senate Committee on Commerce in Relation to Certain Bills Referred to that Committee Proposing Congressional Regulation of Interstate Commerce,* p. 16, U.S. Government Printing Office, Washington, D.C. (1882).

[100] *id.*, p. 256.

[101] As Senator George of Mississippi pointed out:

> "At the formation of the Constitution the means of transportation and intercourse in interstate commerce mainly consisted in the navigation of our rivers, lakes and the ocean on our borders. That this navigation should be free, free to all, free to an open and unrestricted competition by all, was one of the main and most beneficial ends sought to be attained by the Constitution." (*id.*, p. 12.)

[102] Morison and Commager, *Growth of the Republic,* p. 184.

[103] *Our National Inland Waterways Policy,* an address by President Theodore Roosevelt in Memphis, Tennessee, October 4, 1907.

[104] Joseph Ransdell, "Program for Improvement of American Waterways," *Annals of the American Academy of Political and Social Science,* Vol. XXXI, p. 45, 1908.

[105] "Use and Development of American Waterways," *ibid.,* p. 50. Senator Newlands also pointed out that the debilitated condition of waterway transportation on the Mississippi was the result of two causes:

> "The terrific competition of the railroads, which have made a practice of underbidding the waterways during the navigation season and afterward raising their rates; and also to the failure of the Government to provide and maintain a stable, navigable channel." (*ibid.,* p. 55.)

[106] *ibid.,* p. 56.

[107] *ibid.,* p. 59. The policy of Federal improvement of inland waterways complemented by a prohibition against tolls and operating charges was reaffirmed in the Rivers and Harbors Appropriations Act of 1909. Section 6 of this act of March 3, 1909 (35 Stat. 818) amended Section 4 of the 1884 act to provide for replacement of navigation structures and provided that any navigation improvements thenceforth acquired or constructed by the United States would also be free of tolls and operating charges, except the Panama Canal.

[108] Senator Newlands at pp. 59, 60 "Use and Development of American Waterways." *op. cit.,* Note 105.

The Presidentially appointed Inland Waterway Commission reported that:

> "It was unregulated railroad competition which prevented or destroyed the development of commerce on our inland waterways. The Mississippi, our greatest natural highway, is a case in point. At one time the traffic upon it was without rival in the country. The report shows that commerce was driven from the Mississippi by the railroads." (S. Doc., 325, 60th Congress, 1st Session, 1907)

[109] William Howard Taft expressed the point of view of the Executive Branch on this matter in a Special Message of January 14, 1910:

". . . But it is certain that enormous quantities of merchandise are transported over the rivers and canals in Germany, France, and England, and it is also certain that the existence of such methods of traffic materially affects the rates which the railroads charge, and it is the best regulation of those rates that we have, not even excepting the governmental regulation of the Interstate Commerce Commission. For this reason, I hope that this Congress will take such steps that it may be called the inaugurator of the new system of inland waterways."

[110] See notes 103, 104, 105.

[111] *A Water Policy for the American People,* Vol. 1, p. 204, Government Printing Office, Washington, D.C., 1950.

[112] President Warren G. Harding also voiced the hope that water and rail transportation could be coordinated and that the railroads would help facilitate such coordination.

[113] Acceptance Address, August 14, 1924. During his term of office, President Calvin Coolidge reiterated his interest in aiding the farmer through the provision of cheap transportation:

"The large Federal expenditure for improvement of waterways and highways in all comprise a great series of governmental actions in the advancement of the special interest of agriculture." (Fourth Annual Message, December 7, 1926.)

"The Inland Waterways Corporation is proving successful and especially beneficial to agriculture." (Fifth Annual Message, December 6, 1927.)

[114] Representative Briggs of Texas enumerated many of these economic benefits and pointed out that not the least of them would be the increased purchasing power which the farmer would have as a result of more efficient marketing of his goods. (*Congressional Record,* 69th Congress, 1st Session, p. 10656, 1926.)

[115] *Congressional Record,* 68th Congress, 2nd Session, p. 1890, 1925.

[116] *ibid.,* p. 1916.

[117] *ibid.,* p. 1930. In similar debates in 1926, Lozier told the House:

"The people of eleven great States want to cooperate in the development of a great inland waterway system which will furnish cheap transportation and contribute tremendously to the development of the agricultural interests of the great West." (*Congressional Record,* 69th Congress, 1st Session, P. 10664, 1926.)

[118] *ibid.* Emphasis upon protection of the waterways from the destructive "what-the-traffic-will-bear" rate policies of the railroads was vigorously renewed during this era. Representative Colton of Utah, while arguing for more effective "long and short haul" regulation during these debates, reminded his colleagues that waterway improvements could not provide optimum benefits to the Nation's economy, until the railroads were pre-

vented from establishing rates designed to destroy water transportation. (*ibid.*, p. 1918.)

[119] Speech of Secretary of Commerce Herbert Hoover, St. Louis, Missouri, November 14, 1927. Hoover also shared Congress' view that the modernization of the Nation's waterway system would, by decreasing shipping costs, increase the price of all grain to the farmer by 10 cents per bushel. He, also, felt that a single year of such increase to our Midwest farmers would more than equal the entire proposed outlay.

[120] *ibid.*

[121] President Hoover's speech at Louisville, Kentucky, in October 1929, appearing in the *Congressional Record,* Senate Section, October 24, 1929.

[122] *Congressional Record,* 74th Congress, 1st Session, p. 5252, 1935. In making this speech on the floor, Representative Mansfield echoed the opinion expressed in House Report 424 of the 74th Congress, 1st Session, 1935, which stated:

> "The projects in this bill — Rivers and Harbors Authorization Bill, 1935 — provide a definitely rounded-out plan for the continued improvement of our important rivers and harbors to meet changes in navigation and commercial conditions and demand the approval of Congress for their establishment to insure a reasonably progressive and comprehensive development in accordance with the long-established policy of Congress."

[123] *id.,* pp. 5265-68. Representative Colden also gave a detailed example (*id.,* p. 5267) to demonstrate what a good friend cheap waterway transportation is to the farmer.

[124] Speech of Secretary of Commerce Hoover, St. Louis, Missouri, November 14, 1927.

[125] *Congressional Record,* 74th Congress, 1st Session, p. 5257, 1935.

[126] *ibid.* Representative Colden (see footnote 123) also cited Pittsburgh and Chicago as examples of areas where improved water transportation facilities had aided in the development of railroad centers. Representative Mansfield of Texas explained the reason for these increases in rail transportation in areas of improved waterway facilities during his introduction of the 1935 Rivers and Harbors Appropriations Bill in these terms:

> "Reasonable but substantial reduction in freight rates is one of our greatest possible needs. The low cost of water transportation on the Great Lakes, of about 1 mill per ton-mile, has added many billions to the economic wealth of the Country and has actually contributed more to the business of the railroads . . . than perhaps any single development in our history. . . . It is a fact that cannot be denied that the railroads which operate in the same zones where the greatest volume of waterway traffic is handled are the most prosperous roads we have. . . . We find that in 1900 in the Pittsburgh district the traffic on the Allegheny, Monongahela and Ohio rivers was 9,000,000 tons. In 1925, it had increased to 40,000,000 tons and here is how it affected the railroads. In 1900, the rail traffic was 57,000,000 tons and in 1925 it had increased to 173,000,000 tons. . . .

"The cheap movement of raw materials resulted in building up the greatest industrial region on the American continent and provided a greater volume of traffic to move by rail than is to be found in any other section of our country." *Congressional Record,* 74th Congress, 1st Session, p. 5251.

Representative Eckert (Pa.) (*ibid.,* p. 5265) concurred in this statement.

[127] *ibid.,* p. 5264. With regard to governmental improvement of rivers and harbors in general, Eckert then stated:

". . . all agree that the improvement of rivers and harbors is an obligation of government. Rivers and harbors are commerce and trade channels, and it is a function of government to provide public thoroughfares on land and water for the use and convenience of the people. This is a well-settled principle of American jurisprudence. Therefore, the Federal Government is well within its rights in improving at public expense the rivers and harbors of the nation." (*ibid.*)

[128] *ibid.*

[129] *ibid.,* p. 5254.

[130] *ibid.,* p. 5253.

[131] Discussing the contribution of the inland waterway system to the war effort, the President's Water Resources Policy Commission said:

"The service rendered by inland waterway transportation during World War II demonstrated conclusively that it is a vital instrument of national defense. Its performance in contributing toward the winning of the war more than justified the confidence of the Congress in the Corps of Engineers' waterway improvement program prosecuted for and sponsored by the people, and more than repaid the Federal Government for all of the expenditures of public funds for that program." (*A Water Policy for the American People,* Vol. 1, p. 424.)

And the Office of Defense Transportation stated:

"If our waterways rendered no service beyond that of transporting petroleum and its products during the war, they would have amply justified their improved existence." (*ibid.*)

[132] *Congressional Record,* 84th Congress, 2nd Session, p. 12056, 1956. This sense of tradition has been expressed on numerous other occasions since 1946. In 1946, Representative Johnson of California said:

"Since the inception of our Government, it has been the policy to develop streams by widening, straightening and deepening them and thus encourage the use of water transportation." (*Congressional Record,* 79th Congress, 2nd Session, p. 6265, 1946.)

The 1949 Report of the House Public Works Committee on the Rivers and Harbors Authorization Bill stated:

"Since 1824 the Congress has wisely fostered a sound and progressive development of our rivers and harbors in the interest of foreign and domestic commerce." (81st Congress, 1st Session, House Report 969, 1949.)

A similar report by the same committee in 1954 reiterated that:

"The waterway transportation system of the United States is a Federal responsibility stemming from the beginning of the Nation." (83rd Congress, 2nd Session, House Report 2247, 1954.)

[133] 83rd Congress, 2nd Session, House Report 2247, p. 3, 1954.

[134] *Congressional Record*, 84th Congress, 2nd Session, p. 12080, 1956.

[135] *Congressional Record*, 87th Congress, 2nd Session, p. 21867-68, 1962.

[136] *ibid.*, pp. 21868-69.

Members of Congress have continued to base their support of improvement of low-cost water transport facilities on the benefits directly rendered by such improvements to producers, farmers and consumers. Moreover, they have continued to take cognizance of the beneficial effects waterway transportation has rendered as the primary means of keeping rail freight charges at reasonable levels. Representative Mack of Washington effectively expressed this opinion of Congress in 1956 when he argued:

"We must keep our rivers and harbors which are the highways for low-cost cargo shipments in good condition in order that freight charges may be kept low. Whatever reduces transportation costs in the end reduces consumer prices." (*Congressional Record*, 84th Congress, 2nd Session, p. 12060, 1956.)

As it had in the 1930's, Congress has continued to criticize the opposition of the railways to waterway improvements. Senator Barkley of Kentucky criticized the position of the railroads in 1946 in the following manner:

"Of course the railroads do not want the project (Big Sandy River). As a rule they have opposed river improvements – I think under a very mistaken policy. If that attitude had been pursued throughout the Country, we would never have had any river improvements. As a matter of fact rail transportation has not been impaired by river improvements and in many cases it has benefited thereby." (*Congressional Record*, 2nd Session, p. 8311, 1946.)

In a speech during these debates, Senator Overton of Louisiana called the arguments opposing waterway improvements, "nothing more than the old, worn-out railroad opposition to rivers and harbors projects." (*id.* at 8318.)

The overwhelming rejection by Congress of such opposition through its repeated enactment of river and harbor improvements legislation in accordance with established principles, clearly indicates the determination of Congress to maintain the toll-free status of the Nation's waterways in order to assure the economic benefits intended to be provided by the Congressional program of improving these waterways.

In 1948, Senator Overton argued in support of the toll-free waterway policy by reminding his colleagues that:

"There is no policy which is more thoroughly embedded in our national life than the policy of no tolls on any waterways within the jurisdiction of the United States. That policy was established in the very dawn of the Nation. . . I doubt seriously that our great western development could have ever been accomplished if the leaders of that day had been so blind as to have insisted upon or allowed the imposition of tolls on those streams." (*Congressional Record*, 80th Congress, 2nd Session, p. 760, 1948.)

[137] NEWSLETTER published September 6, 1966, by National Waterways Conference, Inc., Washington, D.C.

[138] *ibid.*

[139] 89th Congress, 2nd Session, House Report 2044, 1966.

[140] 83rd Congress, 2nd Session, House Report 1215, 1954.

[141] *Congressional Record*, 84th Congress, 2nd Session, p. 12050, 1956.

[142] *Congressional Record*, 86th Congress, 1st Session, pp. 13598-13600,.1959.

[143] *Congressional Record*, 87th Congress, 2nd Session, p. 21877, 1962.

[144] For an excellent discussion of the possible ramifications of this legislation and the constitutional issues raised by it, see the memorandum by Thomas J. O'Toole, Professor of Law, Georgetown University Law Center, pp. 16285 to 16289, Congressional Record, 88th Congress, 2nd Session, 1964.

[145] *Congressional Record*, 88th Congress, 2nd Session, p. 16299, 1964.

[146] *ibid.*, p. 16300.

[147] *ibid.*, p. 16299.

[148] Beginning with President Franklin D. Roosevelt's Budget Message of January 4, 1940, the Budget Messages of recent Presidents have generally supported a policy of user charges on federally provided facilities. Thus, in President Roosevelt's message above mentioned, it was recommended that "some part" of the annual expenditures for "dredged channels, buoys, lighthouses, life saving stations, etc." be recovered in the form of "small fees" "from users of our lakes, channels and coasts."

President Truman's Budget Messages were generally favorable to extension of user charges to federally provided facilities. President Eisenhower spoke of recovery of expenditures from "those directly benefiting therefrom." The Commerce Department, under Secretary Mueller, in its Report of 1960 entitled *Federal Transport Policy and Program*, recommended waterway user charges in the form of a fuel tax. President Kennedy, in his Budget Messages of 1962 and 1963 and in his Transportation Message of 1962 proposed the institution of a system of user charges on inland waterways by means of a fuel tax of 2 cents per gallon. President Johnson reiterated this proposal in his Budget Messages of 1964, 1965, 1966 and again in 1967. The specific coverage of this 2-cent per gallon tax proposal was stated in a letter from Secretary of the Treasury Douglas Dillon to the Speaker of the House under date of April 13, 1964. Mr. Dillon said the proposed fuel tax would extend to all domestic vessels having a maximum draft of 15 feet or less, exempting vessels in foreign trade or in trade between the Atlantic and Pacific ports, or between the U.S. and its possessions, or in whaling or commercial fishing. Identical coverage was proposed in President Johnson's Message to Congress of May 17, 1965, dealing with excise tax reductions and user charge increases and submitting draft legislation, and in a joint letter to Congress from the Secretaries of Treasury and Commerce under date of March 21, 1966, recommending increased user charges for highways and airways as well as new user charges for waterways.

[149] *Congressional Record,* 88th Congress, 2nd Session, pp. 20573-4, 1964.

[150] Address before the National Waterways Conference, Inc., December 11, 1964, Memphis, Tennessee. Congressional Record, 89th Congress, 1st Session, pp. 972, 973.

[151] Address before the Ohio Valley Improvement Association, October 20, 1965, Cincinnati, Ohio.

[152] Address before the National Waterways Conference, Inc., December 10, 1964, Memphis, Tennessee.

[153] Address before the Mississippi Valley Association, February 8, 1965, St. Louis, Missouri.

[154] Address before the Mississippi Valley Association, February 7, 1966, Washington, D.C.

[155] Remarks at a Panel Discussion on Water Resources Legislation, Annual Convention of the National Rivers and Harbors Congress, June 10, 1966, Washington, D.C.

[156] Address before the Gulf Intracoastal Canal Association, October 24, 1966, New Orleans, Louisiana.

[157] Address before the National Waterways Conference, Inc., November 9, 1966, Little Rock, Arkansas.

[158] Address before the National Waterways Conference, Inc., November 10, 1966, Little Rock, Arkansas.

[159] The text of the resolution opposing waterway user charges, adopted unanimously by the Southern Governors' Conference in September, 1966, at Kentucky Dam Village, Kentucky, is as follows:

> "WHEREAS, the development of the water resources of the Nation for water supply, flood control, low-flow augmentation, pollution abatement, recreation, navigation and other essential public purposes is urgently required in the national interest; and
>
> "WHEREAS, future economic progress in the South, including rehabilitation of Appalachia and other depressed areas, is directly dependent upon continued development of its water resources in accordance with policies tested by experience and adequate for emerging needs; and
>
> 'WHEREAS, modern, low-cost water transportation is a major stimulus to industrial growth and associated employment opportunities, of particular importance to the South where the bulk of the Nation's inland waterway commerce originates or terminates; and
>
> "WHEREAS, in reliance upon the long established toll-free waterways policy of the United States, dating from the Northwest Ordinance of 1787 and the Southwest Ordinance of 1790, vast investments of public and private funds have been made in navigation improvements, industrial development, floating equipment and related shore installations; and
>
> "WHEREAS, navigation elements of multi-purpose water resource projects and of comprehensive river basin development programs

contribute substantially to the economic justification of other elements of such projects and programs, such as water supply, flood control, low-flow augmentation, pollution abatement and recreational opportunities; and

"WHEREAS, the imposition of tolls or user charges upon the inland waterways would inevitably reduce waterway traffic and consequently diminish the benefits properly attributable to navigation, thus endangering the economic justification of some multi-purpose projects and comprehensive programs, and placing an undue economic burden on other water resource objectives of all such projects and programs; and

"WHEREAS, discriminatory and destructive waterway tolls or user charges, involving a radical reversal of long established free waterways policy and consequent impairment of existing investments and future growth prospects, have repeatedly been proposed;

"NOW, THEREFORE, BE IT RESOLVED that the Southern Governors' Conference records its opposition to waterway tolls or user charges in any form or in any amount and recommends firm adherence to long established national free waterways policy as an effective instrument in serving vital objectives of public policy such as economic growth, regional rehabilitation and sound development of the Nation's water resources; and

"BE IT FURTHER RESOLVED that the Southern Governors' Conference go on record as endorsing wholeheartedly the resolution entitled 'Inland Navigation Projects,' adopted by the National Governors' Conference at Los Angeles in July, 1966, and relating to standards and criteria for determining navigation benefits; and

"BE IT FURTHER RESOLVED that the Chairman of the Southern Governors' Conference be directed to appoint a Committee on Inland Navigation, with general jurisdiction in this field, which committee shall report to the next annual meeting."

The States represented were Maryland, Delaware, Virginia, West Virginia, North Carolina, South Carolina, Georgia, Florida, Alabama, Mississippi, Louisiana, Arkansas, Oklahoma, Tennessee, Kentucky, Missouri and Texas.

[160] See Note 73.

Index

76

78

About the Authors

WILLIAM J. HULL, a native of Ohio, is a well known attorney practicing in Washington, D. C., and specializing in law relating to water resource development. For many years, he has served as legislative consultant for the Ohio Valley Improvement Association and as secretary of the National Waterways Conference, Inc. A frequent lecturer on water resource topics, he has A.B. and LL.B. degrees from Yale University.

During the preparation of the manuscript, which took nearly 18 months, Mr. Hull was assisted by his son, Robert W. Hull, who served as principal researcher. He holds an A.B. degree from Yale University and an M.A. from Johns Hopkins University.